DANCING IN THE STRATOSPHERE

Memoirs of an American Bomber Pilot

By

Major Frank D. Szachta,

USAF (Retired)

With

Wendell W. Thorne

TITLE Copyright © 2015 by Frank D. Szachta

Book and Cover design by Chuck Szachta www.chuckszachta.com

ISBN-13: 978-1516987306

ISBN-10: 1516987306

First Edition: August 2015

I wish to dedicate this book to Nedra. Once she came into my life in 1951, she immediately became a key player and partner that made my life "click". She was the vital companion in raising our family, and was fundamental to all the success I ever had in aviation, in raising our children, and all facets of my life. I could not have had nearly the happiness, achievement, or any other aspect of my life, or that of our children, without her presence in my life. She was the foundation of my life in all ways. I miss her very much, and have found myself struggling since her death. I thank the Lord for having brought us together in our wartime romance, and the many joyful years we had together. She is and always will be the heroine of my story.

ACKNOWLEDGMENTS

I'd like to thank my family in Buffalo, including my mother that died when I was very young; my Father who raised us last five children by himself; my brothers and sisters (all 10 of them) since all of them played a part in our early years of life; of course my wife Nedra who was so large a part of our family's strength; our six children, who were so important to our family's success due to Nedra's great upbringing of them all; my two high school teachers, Mr. Fliss and Ductor, who were instrumental in a super high school education and introduction into my life in Aviation; and a host of friends we made during our Air Force career. I must also include many of our friends in St. Louis, where we lived for over 28 years after the Air Force. The Buckley family of Mike and Gael and the Burger family of Bill and Mary Anne who were close neighbors for many years. They were both very close friends to Nedra and I for over 25 years. We had numerous neighborhood parties with both, and loved them dearly. There are many other friends we had over the years and we appreciated their friendship and help over our many years of fellowship.

INTRODUCTION

Frank Szachta is not a tall man. At 5 feet, five inches, he was the shortest boy child in his family of ten. He is 84 years old now, so you may think he's shrunk over the years. No. He's always been challenged, vertically speaking.

But in the eyes of his late wife and six children, he was a giant. Also, in the eyes of nearly everyone who met him. Born and raised in the Polish section of Buffalo, New York during the Great Depression, one could understand if his dreams had remained just that: Dreams. After all, when hot running water or a new (used) pair of shoes is considered luxury, becoming a pilot and traveling the world seems as likely as building a skyscraper by hand or walking to Jupiter.

But Frank was born with...*something*. A beautiful mind that could not abide the notion of "failure"? Perhaps. A sense of naiveté that could scarcely comprehend personal limitations? Possibly. Or, perhaps it is simply an example of something known as "Napoleon Syndrome"; the instinctive drive of the diminutive to publicly—and in no small way—avenge what to them is a simple cruelty of birth.

Whatever it is—and, at the conclusion of this book the reader is more than welcome to formulate his or her own theory—Frank Szachta defied odds, an understatement if ever there were one.

I first met Frank Szachta when he walked into my barbershop in Ellenton, Florida last summer (like all but the slim minority of writers, I have a day job). My shop is situated in a 100-year old building with high ceilings, suspended from which are a number of large-scale remote controlled airplanes. Being a pilo, I enjoy having airplanes and aviation-related mementos in my shop. Frank noticed the yellow J-3 Piper Cub and we began to chat as I wrestled with his unruly coif. Having had a brush with military aviation myself, I'm always both respectful and highly interested in the stories of those who flew the great military aircraft of yesterday. Admittedly unfamiliar with the B-47 Stratojet, I nevertheless listened carefully as he spoke of his missions in the great bomber and her potentially devastating cargo. Even at age 84, Frank had not forgotten a single airspeed, system or procedure related to the Cold War's first line of defense (until, at least, the advent of the workhorse B-52). Frank easily related stories and anecdotes as I

----

trimmed—and listened. Soon it became evident that the man had had a remarkable life.

But his book isn't just about Frank. Couldn't be. For, without Nedra, his now late wife of 61years, the story of Frank Szachta would probably not have been very interesting or noteworthy. It is said that behind every great man is a great woman. Nedra wasn't *behind* anybody. Nedra was *beside* Frank—occasionally *ahead*—every step of the way. The bond they formed early on lead to a sense of sacrifice and commitment that, like those houses constructed of Florida Dade County Pine, time only strengthened. Together—a word that, in this case really has little to do with *physical* togetherness—they blazed a trail through life, brought six children into this world, made countless life-long friends, learned lessons and taught them right back.

This book is a love story. Real love; not that stuff you hear on the radio or see on T.V. Real love is solid, unwavering and forward-moving. But this story is also a testament to a time when great nations behaved like schoolyard children playing a game of Truth or Dare. When rapidly-changing technology created the unfathomable possibility that the world could be destroyed by the push of a button. When brave men (not women yet) rose to the call, took to the skies and did their level best to outfox what we now know was an equally puzzled rival; for a military man, fighting the Cold War was like trying to lasso smoke.

Frank Szachta didn't notice that it was difficult,

scoffing at the word "impossible". A man of faith, secure in himself and, more importantly, in the young woman with moxie who shared his enthusiasm for life, Frank was asked to do something, and he did it. He calls himself "lucky." Says he's "blessed."

In reality, he was just being Frank.

And you'll hear his story largely in his own words. His *side* of the story, anyway. Frank and Nedra's children will provide their own take on the events, tales, struggles and joys going on "stateside", even though the family carried through with their vow to stay together whenever possible; sadly, busy dads living in the house can get preoccupied and miss things. You'll hear some of what Nedra had to say about all this as well.

Those who can in the Szachta family will tell you theirs was like any other military family; that they ran into no serious life trauma or financial setbacks, or much health-related difficulty. But set against the backdrop of the onset of grand changes in American life and an earthquake of upheaval in the American family, the Szachta family persevered and, as a team, they overcame the odds.

You will also read what Frank and Nedra's friends have to say about them, both as a couple and as individuals, for that is what they are. Were. Two strong individuals taking up the challenge of the American dream and making it look easy.

But, it *wasn't* easy. It was difficult because it's

---

supposed to be difficult. If the life they lived and the accomplishments they achieved were easy, everybody'd do it.

This book should be required reading for every newly married couple, or those seeking to become so. It is a road map for the journey of life, founded in mutual respect, admiration, and abject, complete and unending love.

The way it's supposed to be.

WWT

CHAPTER ONE:

LUCKY SEVEN

To say that 1930 was a difficult year for most Americans is perhaps the understatement of that century. The events set in motion when the New York Stock Exchange crashed on Tuesday, October 29, 1929 caused a series of bank runs that resulted in a domino effect of failed banks across the United States. Investors lost billions. Factories, mills, mines and shipyards shut down, or severely cut back their workforces. The fallout affected shops, dealerships, gas stations, restaurants, and those supplying services, like barbershops and dry cleaners. Unemployment rose to 30 per cent. Much of America was at a financial standstill with no hope of any speedy relief.

In fact, the years since the turn of the century had been a roller-coaster of relative prosperity and serious economic downturn. Mini "depressions," what we now refer to as recessions, came along regularly, as the nation struggled with finding a balancing point, a place of measured economic growth, industrial expansion, diminishing agricultural dependency, and political and social discovery. During the first quarter of the twentieth century, Buffalo basked in relative prosperity, despite the uneasiness and instability that simmered in the other parts of the nation.

After the crash of 1929, however, things were no different for Buffalo, despite the grand city's once admired status as one of the most diversified economic giants of the Rust Belt. Buffalo had been fortunate due, in large part, to its location. Thanks to the Erie Canal, everything from grain to steel flowed into and out of Buffalo, making it the ideal place to manufacture automobiles, airplanes, chemicals, and rubber. The invention of Joseph Dart's grain elevator revolutionized the process of shipping wheat, greatly streamlining a once labor-intensive task.

In the decade that followed the crash, Buffalo's economy was devastated as industries came to a virtual standstill, her half-million-plus citizens suddenly thrust from prosperity to poverty. For Americans everywhere, it had to have been the unluckiest time to begin life.

Having no say in the matter however, Francis David Szachta (pronounced "Zackta") was born on June 3, 1930. The eighth child of Rose (Kacmierczak) and Francis Raymond Szachta (the offspring would one day total ten), Frank entered an uncertain world, to say the least. Diminutive in stature and precocious in nature, Frank's curious spirit consumed the world around him as if drinking from a fire hydrant. As one of ten children whose father eked out a meager existence as a railroad laborer, Frank knew nothing of prosperity. For that matter, he could not be bothered with the concept of poverty. He lived his life, was cared for in the way of his siblings and others in the neighborhood, and had no experience with divisions within the socio-economic classes. That characteristic was altered somewhat when Frank was eight years old. In the Polish ethnic section of Buffalo, things had not improved for most, but as Frank celebrated his eighth Christmas, his eyes were opened somewhat.

During the Christmas season of 1938, I remember going north on Miller Avenue toward Sycamore street to a friend's house to watch him play with his model train set. It was hard for us to imagine anyone so rich that they had such a grand train set to play with at Christmastime. We never had a bike, or any large toys, and it wasn't until the forties that I remember us making a scooter out of an orange crate, a 2x4 board and a set of roller skate wheels. We played with the train set for a couple of hours, and I recall visiting him several more times during the holiday season. I think his family was the richest one we knew on Miller

Avenue.

However, living for years with no real benchmark to gauge their economic status—being children, Frank and at least the younger siblings were naturally insulated from money issues—young Frank had little or no knowledge or understanding of finances. In fact, Frank's father, also named Frank ("Pa"), worked as a union railroad laborer with the New York Central Railroad company, likely earning less than $1,000 per year. It is difficult to imagine a family of 12 living off so little, but at least Frank's dad didn't lose his job, as about 40% of his co-workers did, in the Great Depression. When his mother passed away of pleurisy in 1940, the significant task of raising the children was relegated to Pa and the older sisters, Wanda and Eileen, who had already married and left the home.

Of course, us kids had no concept of money yet, and since we knew Pa was a railroad laborer, we didn't know if the $22/month rent was a bargain or not. Since Pa made all such decisions, we figured everything was OK. I do recall that during the early years after Ma's death our older sisters Wanda and Eileen would occasionally bring us some casseroles for supper. Our older sister at home, Lottie, had learned some cooking at Ma's side just before her death, but her suppers were supplemented by the elder sisters' help.

Ignorant of the stresses facing the adults in his community—and in his home—Frank found ways to enjoy his childhood with his friends and siblings. But, moving at breakneck speed through one's early years means you better _have some amount of luck if you're going to survive._

It's 1935 so I must have been about five years old by now. One day we were playing in the small yard at 156 Miller Avenue in Buffalo, N.Y., and, to get away from my friend I darted out into the street between a couple of parked cars. I did not see the car coming from Sycamore Avenue to the north and before I could stop myself or get out of the way, the fender smacked me, and I fell to the street. Ma heard the car bakes screech. The driver jumped out of his car and picked me up. I was unconscious, and was told later that he asked Ma where the nearest doctor was. In those days, doctor's offices were in their homes, and she told him where the nearest one was north to Walden Avenue, two blocks away. The driver laid me on his back seat and the driver asked Ma to come with him to the doctor's office. In a few minutes we were at the doctor's office and by then I was conscious and a bit alert. I complained that my head hurt a little, and I had a few brush burns for hitting the street where I fell. The doctor felt my head, arms and legs all over, and asked me if I was OK. He told Ma to take me home for a rest, and to watch that I didn't fall asleep right away, since that could mean a head injury was causing it. The driver paid the doctor $2 for the office visit and gave Ma and me a ride back home. He was relieved that I wasn't hurt badly and he gave Ma $2 when we got home for the trouble.

Frank's zest for life was not unlike that of any other boy growing up in any city anywhere in America. But with *her hands full of homemaking duties, chronic illness and a houseful of children, Ma didn't need any further stress. Frank, however, seemed to find his share of trouble. On the Fourth of July, 1937, seven-year-old Frank was ready for the Independence Day holiday. Ma had dressed him up in an entirely white outfit! Pants, shirt, coat, shirt, socks and shoes, all white. One has to wonder how an experienced mother—with six prior children and Frank, already—could arrive at the decision to dress a seven-year-old boy all in white, but it is obvious she was astute and had her reasons for so doing. Given the events of that day, there is little doubt that she later questioned that logic. It seems some other kids in the neighborhood,*

"...between ten and twelve years old were lighting and blowing up huge firecrackers in the grass field just east of our house on Miller Avenue. The field was pretty big, and extended across the New York Central railroad tracks that ran east and west past Miller. The firecrackers they were setting off were huge and the noise of their explosions could be heard for blocks. I walked over to the part of the field where the firecrackers were exploding to see if I could get closer to the action.

One gang of kids was putting their huge firecrackers into glass quart milk bottles to make the noise louder. [Dressed in my white outfit] I walked closer to the milk bottle zone, and saw a firecracker in a bottle that hadn't exploded yet. As I got about three feet for the bottle, the firecracker exploded, and there was a large noise as glass from the bottle flew in every direction. The noise hurt my ears, but I did not realize that the flying glass had cut my legs in a couple of places. I guess the pieces of flying glass were so sharp, I didn't even feel them hit me! I looked down and saw the blood start to flow all over my pants and socks, and my first thought was I was in trouble for messing up my nice suit...Ma and my older sister Lottie washed off my legs and put some bandages on the cuts. The cuts were all superficial, but the best stroke of luck was—I didn't even get scolded for getting my new holiday suit all bloody!

Energetic, and with a sense of undeterred curiosity and eagerness to take in all of what life had to offer, Frank had a way of finding himself in situations that could have easily resulted in disaster. Whether a blessing from a guardian angel or simple fortune, Frank usually came out virtually unscathed, physically. Psychological scarring, however, is more difficult to heal.

There was a set of New York Central Railroad tracks just south of our house, and the tracks ran between our house and our grade school, PS #44, which was only two blocks away. I remember during our years on Miller Avenue that we kids would use the stopped trains at the crossing as a perfect excuse for being late for class in the morning— they simply blocked our way to school. Whether the real reason for a slow start to the school day was because we were tardy in getting out of bed, washing up or eating breakfast, the "train excuse" was a tailor-made and believable reason for being late to school. Actually, I was rarely late and quite punctual—and almost never absent. This habit was good for all of us, because, as luck would have it, the teachers always believed that it was the stopped trains that made us late! Eventually, however, the city built a road underpass under the train tracks, and our handy excuse was no more.

But it was these same tracks that were the site of some horrible accidents while I was growing up. We would often walk the rails looking for coal that had fallen from the engine tenders and spilled along the tracks as the trains moved between the Bailey Avenue switchyard and our street. We were always careful to watch for moving trains, since there was little room between two trains passing along the set of rails. The locomotive engines were huge and noisy enough scare us kids off anyway. On occasion, however, other kids would try to hitch a ride on a train just leaving the switchyard for points all over the country, and this is usually when accidents would happen. I remember one such accident, when I walked near the Bailey switchyard, and I looked down for the overpass and saw the sheet laying a cross a boy's body on the tracks. His legs were cut off, and he died right there on the tracks. The sight of that young boy lying there dead on the tracks left an impression on my brain that is there to this day.

But Frank's active childhood behavior was balanced with a sense of artistic creativity and a pure and loving heart. He loved to fashion toys out of odds and ends, and his vision—not his eyesight—was alerted to sensory events

----

that his siblings seemed not to notice. For instance,

After Ma's death, we had to move to a smaller cottage located at 357 Koons Avenue, which was about a ten minute walk northeast of our Miller Avenue house. The smaller house cost only $22 per month, but it had three small bedrooms upstairs with enough room for Pa to raise the five children, including me, who still lived at home. It was still in St. Luke's Catholic parish, but the grade school was PS #62. We asked our sister Wanda, who everybody called, "Winnie" and who lived about four blocks from PS #44 if we could take our lunches at her house, and she agreed, which allowed us to stay at PS#44 where we all— Stan, myself, and Jack—had started our schooling.

Those lunches I remember fondly, as I'm sure it was a big sacrifice for Winnie and her family, and I will never forget that favor. Most of the time, we would walk the few blocks to sister Wanda's for a baloney sandwich and a glass of milk for lunch. Once in a while, Wanda made her famous meatball soup, which was essentially milk gravy with homemade meatballs and peas. One of my special favorites.

The Koons Avenue cottage had a small kitchen, a tiny dining room (that we never ate in) and a small living room. There was also an unheated closet/porch where the wringer washer and tubs were kept. Every Monday, Pa rose early enough to do the washing for a whole week. He'd run the washer and tubs for himself and all us kids, then, in the summer, he'd hang the wash out in the backyard while, in the winter he would hang them in the third floor attic to dry.

All this work and Pa still made it to work by 7A.M. Over the years, I've asked my siblings if they remembered Pa doing this, and none seemed able to recall it. I found this fact mind-boggling, and wondered if each child sees a different set of parents.

Obviously, Frank's early years began to shape his sense of discernment, judgment and discretion, and he exhibited an uncanny ability to absorb the life around him with vision and an innate understanding of people. These are the characteristics that establish the well-roundedness necessary to becoming a U.S. Air Force pilot.

While at PS#44, Frank developed his passion for knowledge, fondly recalling the assistance of his teachers.

The first teacher I remember at all was our third grade teacher, and I recall she helped me a lot. In those years, teachers could not be married, and I remember the term "Old Maid," but I am sure that us young kids did not realize the impact of that policy. In the fourth grade, I remember my teacher was Miss Wohlers, and she helped me with geography and other subjects. I liked geography best of all subjects, and that may explain my love of travel, foreign countries, and all aspects of this enjoyment that has sparked joy into all parts of my life.

School years at PS#44 also unearthed Frank's

---

hidden talents.

I learned to play drums, and I really enjoyed playing, especially after fourth grade. My father spent $55 on a set of drums for me to play on. It seemed like an awful lot of money for him to spend on just one of us kids and it still seems so today. 'Where on earth did he get that kind of money on his small pay as a railroad laborer?,' is what I remember thinking, and to this day I have no idea. In fact, I remember one time Pa told us his union had negotiated a three-cent per hour raise, and that was cause for a family celebration.

I played drums for the next four years at PS#44, mostly in the Drum & Bugle Corps, but also in the school band. Since I was the smallest boy—almost in all the school —the snare drum I played would bang on my knees as we marched along. The school band played as the students came into the auditorium for announcements, plays, and other school activities. I recall our music teacher was a short, heavy lady that was very strict with the band. Since drummers always played the same "notes" I did not learn to read music very well. I preferred to play "freestyle" as the band played the musical selections, rather than the actual written drum part. The music teacher would give me the 'evil eye' as I played my personal renditions of the percussion parts, and often reprimand me afterwards.

One auditorium presentation where I did not get in trouble was a band recital where all the band members got to play a solo performance. I let all my energy flow forth out of me full blast did my best Gene Krupa impression, as he was my drummer idol at the time. I played fast and hard —and loud—and the kids in the audience really seemed to enjoy it. I'm not sure why I didn't pursue drumming in high school, but I guess my poor music reading skills were partly to blame.

A healthy ego is one of the characteristics of all military aviators. It's obvious that Frank very much enjoyed being up on stage and the center of attention. Perhaps he was still trying to overcome a personal attitude over his smaller stature by playing 'big' that day in the PS#44 auditorium. He may have been small, but, like "Rudy" Ruettiger—the diminutive (5' 6") fellow from Joliet, Illinois who dreamed of playing football for Notre Dame—Frank always had a huge heart, which seemed to more than compensate for his lack of physical size.

Speaking of athletics, while at PS#44, Frank discovered that he had a talent for swimming. Lucky for him (again) PS#44 was one of a very few schools in Buffalo to actually have a 20-yard indoor swimming pool. He developed his talent for swimming in the fifth grade, and "was swimming pretty fast by the sixth grade." That was in the freestyle stroke.

Our swim teacher was Mr. Gies, and he was famous for the "Gies Slap," which was a wet towel snap on the buttocks (we swam naked during swim practices). I'm told it was pretty painful, but I guess I was pretty well behaved and disciplined on the swim team and I never was on the receiving end of his towel. Well, at the end of sixth grade, Mr. Gies told me to practice the freestyle stroke all summer so that I could help the swim team next year. But, Frank, being Frank, had other ideas. The butterfly stroke was just starting up as a new swim stroke, and I decided that that stroke was more fun to learn and practice than the freestyle stroke. We lived about a mile for Schiller Park with its outdoor swim and dive pools, and we kids spent almost every day there during the summer of '42.

As the seventh grade swim season began, Mr. Gies had all us boys try out for the team. He was surprised and disappointed (but did not deliver the "Gies Slap" on me) that I'd disobeyed him and practiced the butterfly stroke more that summer. Nevertheless, he gave me a chance, and I made the team with the butterfly. My big day came in the area swim meet, when I placed second in the butterfly event! That was the first time I ever received an award for an athletic event. At the award ceremony in the school auditorium (where I'd wowed them with my drums only a year earlier) I remember Mr. Gies words verbatim as he gave me the silver medal: "Dynamite comes in small packages, but is still very explosive!" I felt like I was six feet tall that day.

As with the drums, I did not follow-up with swimming in high school, but only because Burgard didn't have a swimming pool.

In fact, if Frank had have been six feet tall, this book may have never been written, and Frank's story might have been significantly different.

One area of Frank's life that he had yet to discover— or at least investigate—was the opposite sex. His life to this point had been focused on drinking in the world around him, trying to do well in school, and playtime. When other boys found themselves drawn to girls, Frank was out in the yard, tossing a ball, or in the neighborhood trying—at least a little bit—to stay out of trouble. There is little doubt that Frank had an innate drive to succeed at this thing called life, a virtue that somehow, in his youth, did not involve girls. His older sisters were already out of the house when Frank's memories begin, and his mother was sickly and his Pa was probably much too busy to concern themselves with the topic of Frank and the opposite sex. There is little record of whether older brother Stan ever discussed the topic with his younger brothers.

Even though I was pretty outgoing at PS#44, I met few, if any, girls in school, at least until graduation parties. And even then I was at a loss for how to treat them. I guess my drumming and my swimming were 'boy' centered activities, and I myself was probably quite self-centered, to the point that I was totally naïve around girls.

I do recall one party right after school graduation at a girl's home near Winnie's on Mohr Avenue. There were about six boys and the same number of girls at this party, and they were playing games I'd never heard of—but the girls seemed to know them quite well. One was called "Post Office," where you went into a dark closet with a girl and practiced kissing. We also played "Spin The Bottle," where you had to kiss the girl who spun the bottle, if the neck of the bottle pointed at you when the bottle stopped spinning. I was truly out of my element and, when the song, "Roll Me Over in The Clover" played on the record player, I was overwhelmed with all kinds of new emotions and feelings, what with all the kissing going on. I remember thinking that I was quite naïve and inexperienced—compared to the girls at the party.

With Frank being involved in an entirely different kind of "swimming," his life may have turned out differently had it not been for one significant alteration: He went on to an all-boys high school. With the onslaught of manhood, lots of boys find themselves waylaid on their journey because of the fairer sex; it's only natural, after all. But Frank's good fortune in that area continued to set the stage for what was in store for him, both professionally and personally. While not engaging in the traditional boy/girl issues in high school did trouble him—"I must have been the biggest example of inexperience and naiveté in any person I have ever known, before or since…"—it's possible that his life may have taken a dramatically different pathway under different circumstances. He might have

MAJOR FRANK D. SZACHTA | 26

followed in Pa's footsteps and gone to work at the railroad. Or, he may have stuck with the drums, or perhaps become a teacher and swimming coach. Either way, one thing is relatively certain: He would have never met the girl of his dreams.

CHAPTER TWO: A GIRL NAMED "NEDRA"

Halfway across the country, 1930's St. Louis was affected the same as Buffalo and every other major industrial city in the nation. By 1933 St. Louis had lost half of its manufacturing production output and more than 30% of St. Louis workforce was unemployed. With the start of the Works Progress Administration (WPA), the federal government began creating jobs for displaced workers by having them undertake public beautification and construction programs. Between 1932 and 1936, around $68 million had been spent in relief for St. Louis by governmental agencies, with $50 million from federal, $6 million from state, and $12 million from city sources. The construction of the Jewel Box **in** *Forest Park, Soldier's*

Memorial, Homer G. Phillips Hospital, the Kings highway viaduct, the paving of Lambert Field runways, and the massive removal of forty blocks of the St. Louis riverfront for the Jefferson National Expansion Memorial all received funding from the WPA. As for St. Louis, however, not all of the decade's news was bad. On April 7, 1933, The Cullen-Harrison Act was signed, effectively ending Prohibition, and St. Louis rejoiced. On April 8, Anheuser Busch celebrated by sending a team of Clydesdale horses bearing a gift case of Budweiser beer to the White House.[1]

That same year, Nedra Joan Kimberlin was born to Charlie and Wannie Kimberlin of 2606 Louisiana Avenue, St. Louis, MO. The Great Depression hit the Kimberlins especially hard.

Nedra writes:

My early childhood was not very happy. We were poor, with no electricity, no hot water. This was in a flat in south St. Louis. About 1941, though, things got better when my father got a job at Fred Harvey's[2] Barber Shop. We did okay even though my father drank every night and liked to gamble some. But, my mother never knew how much money my father made until it was tax time. We were

---

[1] "St. Louis Celebrates"; www

[2] Fred Harvey was a nineteenth century entrepreneur who is credited as the inventor of America's first chain restaurant. Serving the Atchison, Topeka and Santa Fe Railway, the Gulf Coast and Santa Fe Railway, the Kansas Pacific Railway, the St. Louis-San Francisco Railway, and the Terminal Railroad Association of St. Louis, "Harvey House" restaurants were prolific even into the 1960's although rail travel in the United States had been in decline for a number of decades. "Milestones: Jun. 18, 1965". *Time.* June 18, 1965

always moving out to a new apartment in the middle of the night.

Nedra's account of an event when she was six years old is most compelling.

One day I was invited to go someplace "rich"—the Kilcullens' house. Their mother bathed me and shampooed my hair, put on a clean dress. My Mom said they put something in my hair, as they were all blondes. At our house, we had no hot water for baths. Just cold water. I had boils on my elbows and knees from poor hygiene. I was six years old at the time. I loved being cleaned up and pretty but I was put down at home. I'm sure my Mom was embarrassed.

Obviously the Depression hit the Kimberlin's home very hard, both in real, tangible terms and in the psychological effect it had on everyone in the family. Nedra's mother relied upon a negative emotional response in the face of what she may have judged to be another family's way of criticizing her own family. It's more likely that the Kilcullens were just reaching out and doing what they could to help out a family in need. Either way, one thing is clear: Nedra had seen how life "on the other side of the tracks" was lived. And she liked it.

Nedra did not have the large family like Frank did, as she had but one older sister and two younger brothers. But she made up for that by making good, life-long friends.

In grade school, there were four of us girls who did

everything together. We had our lunch together every day, and wrote notes to each other, revealing our thoughts and dreams. On Saturdays, we'd go to Tower Grove Park to play ball, etc. We really were inseparable.

As time went on and Nedra's father landed his job at Fred Harvey's barbershop, the family moved on and up. Financially, things improved. The family moved to a nicer apartment. Things change, however, and some are not so good. Soon after the girls started high school, one of the four switched to a private school. Then, another moved and changed schools, leaving just Nedra and Peggy together.

With the other girls gone, it was just Peggy and me. I was a shy, very skinny kid, and Peggy was heavier, with a limp from having had Polio, so the two of us hung together. Peggy was a straight-A student, so I was always trying to keep up with her—consequently I did well in all my classes.

Frank's recollection of the time with the girls at his graduation party—how they seemed so advanced, experienced—doesn't seem to be shared by Nedra. She made no mention of any boy/girl experiences while in high school. Either there were few or none, or future events in her life somehow relegated those times to a less-important place in her memory banks. More likely is that Nedra possessed some of that zest for life that drove Frank.

By my senior (or maybe my junior year) of high school, I got a job at the soda fountain and magazine stand at Union Station. Peggy met a farmer, who was a friend of the family, and got married soon after we graduated high school. But I wasn't thinking about marriage. My family was so proud of me—I am the only one of my siblings to have graduated high school! After graduation in 1951, the "Red Capes"[3] at Union Station kept encouraging me to get a better job. I took their advice and was hired at the Army Finance Center on Goodfellow Boulevard as a typist with a pay grade of GS-2. It wasn't long before I was promoted to a researcher in the Savings Bond Branch—a GS 3, Wow! I spent all my money on *me*!

Absent Nedra's ambition for something more in life, what happened next may have never occurred.

I had lost my friend, Peggy, who was busy with a husband and living in Columbia, Illinois. But as God closed one door, He opened another. A new family moved into our apartment building and they had a daughter about my age, Jane Eckles. Jane and I had a lot of fun together, shopping, etc. She knew some girls who went to the dances at the YWCA downtown, so off we went (although my parents never owned a car, the bus ran only a block from the house, so we had transportation). Jane and I spent a lot of Saturday nights at these dances, and I always danced with a lot of guys, all servicemen. We always had an immense amount of fun at the YWCA dances…

One night, in September of 1951, Nedra's life

---

[3] Porters and Ramp Agents

changed forever…

CHAPTER THREE: THE SHAPING OF A PILOT

His early years now in the rearview mirror, Frank was faced with a decision that would ultimately launch his journey into the air.

After graduation from PS#44, I took the entrance exams for two Vocational/Technical high schools. My first choice was Burgard Vocational High School, because that school trained boys in airplane and engine mechanics, with a post-graduate course to obtain a CAA [now FAA] A&P [Airframe and Powerplant] License. In case I wasn't accepted at Burgard, I also tested the following week for Technical High School in electricity. My brother, Stanley, had gone there and he spoke highly of that school. When I went to test, the teacher's recognized my family name and asked if I was related to Stanley, and I told them he was my older brother. "Well" they said, "we hope you have better attendance habits than he." I found out that Stan had determined the number of school days he could miss and still graduate, and had skipped all those days!

Frank prayed that he would be accepted to Burgard, which he was.

Fortunately for me, I was accepted into the Aviation Program at Burgard and, in September of 1944 I started attending their East Buffalo HS Annex, located a block off of Sycamore and about two miles from our home on Koons Avenue. Ever the competitor, Frank would often run home from school. My schoolmates rode home on the Sycamore streetcar, which stopped every two blocks, and, if I was feeling good, it wasn't too difficult to beat home. My classmates on the streetcar home would cheer or jeer me, depending on how I was faring on that day in my race against the Sycamore streetcar to our home stop.

Burgard Vocational High School was founded in 1910 as a class to teach printing to students from PS#5 and PS#44. In 1914, the school was named Elm Technical School. A $1,000,000 construction project was undertaken on land donated by a local paving contractor named Henry P. Burgard, with the understanding that the school would *bear his name. Founded for the teaching of, primarily, aviation and automobile mechanics and related fields, Burgard had a unique feature of a four-story automobile ramp to move vehicles to the top floor auto shop.* [4]

Appearing to be more of a factory than a school, Burgard was the ideal choice—and a superb starting spot for a career—for Frank Szachta.

The biggest lucky break I had by attending Burgard was having two great teachers named Stan Fliss and Gregory Ductor. They owned a used airplane business and operated it after school hours. The great feature of this was that they would bring damaged planes to school and, under their supervision, we students would repair them and make them flyable again; a great motivational tool for us students to do our best work, that's for sure. But another important aspect of the Fliss/Ductor team was that they would hire students to work for them on weekends and during the summers in their plane repairing business. I worked for them and earned spending money and enough to give Pa a share of my earnings to help pay the family bills. I worked on airplanes all over the Buffalo area, and, with this pay and experience I was able to start flying lessons from Art Siefert at Sheridan Airpark.

Learning to fly an airplane is something everybody ought to endeavor to do. Often described as "easier than driving a car," flying an airplane over the earth is a

---

[4] LaChiusa, C. **Burgard Vocational HS** Retrieved September 19, 2010, from Buffalo Architectural History.

----

tremendously liberating experience, and having the know-how to aviate and navigate an airplane from takeoff to touchdown provides a person with a satisfying sense of accomplishment.

Today's student pilots are somewhat streamlined in a curriculum and flight schedule because many students desire to go on to careers with the airlines. The materials include three-ring binders of information on all facets of flying, FAA Regulations, interactive DVD's, practice exams and the like. On the practical flight side—depending upon the instructor—the elements of flight are taught within a rigid curriculum. Such was not the case in 1946, when Frank—and my own father—began their flying careers. Instructors taught students how to really fly.

Art Seifert owned this combination gas station and airport on Sheridan Drive just west of Transit Road. Since I learned flight principles in our high school courses at Burgard, my flight training went well and I made my first solo flight in August of 1946—after just 5 hours and 50 minutes of flight experience! This was just after I turned 16 years old.

Flying the old, familiar yellow Piper J-3 Cub is embedded in the memories of many post-war flight students. While they were slow and somewhat forgiving, they still had their individual characteristics, and they could surprise an inexperienced pilot.

I recall that each lesson was short, about 20 minutes

in duration, since I didn't have a lot of money for the longer lessons. Since I was studying and learning all about planes and engines in my vocational HS courses at Burgard Vocational HS, the academic side of my lessons were pretty well done before I stepped into the plane. Although my lessons went well, in my recollection, I do have a vivid memory of coming in on final approach one day, and being too high for a good landing. I clearly remember Mr. Siefert saying "you are too high, boy are you high, I have it" as he slipped the plane sideways to drop rapidly into the proper height for landing. One thing I learned that flight was how to aggressively slip a Cub—or any plane—to sink fast, for a good landing, after an approach that was too high.

One other incident I vividly recall involved that same plane. Several pilots had reported to Mr. Siefert that the engine was losing rpm (speed) in flight. He would take the plane for a test hop-, loop it, and do all sorts of maneuvers to try to display the engine problem to no avail. One day, with my few hours of solo experience I decided to try the plane out to find the engine problem the other pilots were reporting. To my surprise, the engine rpm drop from 2500rpm on take-off to about 1500 rpm at 300 feet altitude. To say I was shook-up and a bit afraid is an understatement. I crept around the field traffic pattern, using very shallow banks-, to use all the lift I could get from the slow speed this low engine power was providing me at this time. I landed at once, and white as a ghost, I am sure, and very glad to be safely on the ground again. After this close call, Mr. Siefert had us remove the engine rocker box covers for a look-see.

We found that one cylinder was not getting any lubrication to the rocker arms for the valve operation, and this yielded the loss of power. We cleaned all the oil passages to these boxes, and the engine ran fine thereafter.

Frank learned early, however, that airplane emergencies do not only occur in the air.

Between my sophomore and junior years at Burgard HS I was working during the summer for Mr. Fliss and Ductor. They were my teachers and mentors during HS and we repaired planes in their business as after school partnership.

During July Mr. Ductor was welding on a plane fuselage in a large barn near the Military Road airport in North Tonawanda, NY The fuselage had been damaged, and we pulled the fabric back a bit to clear the weld repair zone. My job was to stand-by with a pail of water as a "fireguard" while Mr. Ductor did the welding. I watched as he welded to be sure that the welding sparks didn't ignite the flammable doped fabric nearby. There were more oil and dope barrels in the barn, quite an incendiary building.

When Mr. Ductor was nearly done, I decided it was nearly all clear, so I put on welding goggles to observe his welding technique. Welding classes start next year for me, and I tried to get a head start on the lessons. What I didn't realize was that as soon as I put on the welding goggles I wouldn't be able to see the low temperature fabric fire, if it started. A few minutes later his partner Mr. Fliss walked into the hangar and hollered "Your Planes on Fire." In a flash Mr. Ductor and I whipped off our welding goggles just in time to see the fuselage fabric was all ablaze. Without a moment's hesitation we picked up the tail of the plane and wheeled it out of the barn before the oil and dope barrels caught fire too. Needless to say, Mr. Ductor chewed me out badly for my poor judgment in putting on the welding goggles and neglecting my job as fireguard. They still let me work for them and I really learned a lifelong lesson.

Ten years later my nephew Joe Licursi followed my footsteps into aviation at Burgard HS. I visited Joe about three years later and he asked me if I heard about the vivid story Mr. Ductor told his welding classes about a fireguard named "Shorty". I had to admit that, not only had I heard the story, I was the Shorty in the story.

In every facet of everything Frank endeavored, he was paying attention, garnering small details and nuances about the experience, evidence of both his logical scientific and creatively artistic mind.

Another pilot experience I recall from those early days of my flying exploits involved a man named Johnny. He owned a PT-19 Fairchild training plane of WWII vintage. It was a low wing plane with plywood wings, and tube and fabric fuselage and tail elements. He used it for acrobatic practice (now called aerobatics). He got it for a very low price, as war surplus, as many so called "War birds" were bought during that period. He invited me for a flight with him one day, and this was a special treat. We wore parachutes for this acrobatic flight, since they were more dangerous than a normal training flight was. This was my first experience with the use of parachutes for flight. We took off in this twin open cockpit plane and proceeded to slowly climb to about 10,000 feet to start our aero rolls and spins. We did about five or six maneuvers I recall till he pulled up level again. We were now down to tree top level, and I was surprised how quickly we lost all that altitude. I found out from him later, that the engine on his PT-19 was about worn-out, and that he couldn't afford an engine overhaul, so he just flew it in its sluggish state.

That and one other flight, in an AT-6 Texan Training plane would be the sum of my early teen-ager flying days of experience. A smattering, but it would serve me well, when my later USAF flying seriously began.

Frank found the flying to be fun and a great adventure, but it was relatively expensive and, in the face of other interests—including acquiring a car and, perhaps a girl to ride along—the job at the airplane repair facility simply didn't pay enough. A job at a service station—the Gulf station on Bailey Avenue, next to the Ideal Bowling Alley—represented a 50% increase in pay, and the added benefit of providing a place to work on his own car—when and if he acquired one. Although the service station was only about a half-hour walk from home, a teenaged boy's mind eventually turns to the idea of owning a car.

The first car I bought was a 1937 Ford with a small V-8 engine. It had a rusted out body and was in poor

---

mechanical condition, but you didn't notice such defects when it's your first car. It could get up to about 55 MPH, but the dirt flew at you through the rusted floorboards at that speed!. But it was fast, and that's all I cared about. I repaired the gas filler pipe and other rusted spots the best I could on a shoestring budget, and my friends and I had fun cruising around Buffalo in my first jalopy—a fair name for this car.

Life for a young man in Buffalo in 1946 was not too shabby, and the proximity of the Ideal Bowling Lanes next to the Gulf station beckoned young Frank and his friends. Back then, bowling lanes had no mechanical pin setting devices such as in today's modern bowling centers. Back then, humans working behind the scenes set pins up for bowlers, and Frank noticed that these pinsetters were paid pretty well, somewhere in the vicinity of $2.50 per hour. Additionally, pinsetters could bowl free—except for the 10 cents they had to pay the other pinsetter—however, the free bowling had to be after leagues, usually late at night or weekends. Nevertheless, Frank changed jobs again, learned to bowl pretty well, and started making about $30 per week as a five-day-a-week pinsetter, "huge pay for a 17-year-old high school junior." One additional benefit: Frank's bowling improved. A development that had, no doubt, something to do with Frank's inherent competitive streak.

One night, halfway through the bowling season, a team in the Ideal Classic League—the top notch scratch league in all of Buffalo, was short a bowler and asked me if

I could sub. I told them I'd have to find someone to sub for my pin setting duties, which I did. While I was honored to be invited to sub for such a team, I was a little intimidated. Well, luck was with me that night (what else is new?) and I ended up bowling a 241, a 245, and another 241, for my lifetime best series of 727. In fact, I only lost the high series for the year in that league by one pin! That series gave me a league average of 199. As a result, I figured I could win the Peterson Classic Bowling Tournament in Chicago, so I went down there by bus and was surprised to see that a 185 series average won the grand prize last year. I automatically figured I could get hot for this one series, just as I did for the Ideal Classic.

I was dead wrong.

As a novice, I didn't realize that they make the alleys a lot slicker for the tournament, and use heavier pins. As a result, it was a rude awakening when my big hook slid straight down the slick alley such that a one-three pocket hit yielded an 8-10 split nearly every time. I returned home, humbled by a 145 average for the tournament. It was a difficult but important lesson I needed to learn.

There was another.

Frank drew a lucky card when he attended an all-boy high school, Burgard, as that decision—along with a healthy respect for his mentors Mr. Fliss and Mr. Ductor—kept him essentially too busy to mess around with girls during his high school years. That, and the fact that he

----

didn't have a car. But, after high school, Frank got his car and he started to investigate this area of his life. As a result of that experience—and the wisdom to listen to the advice of his elders—Frank remained focused on the future.

As mentioned earlier, my meeting girls and kissing them were absent during high school. Afterward, however, with a car available, I started to meet girls again. I recall one young girl what taught me how to kiss. Passionately! I would visit her when she was babysitting a neighbor's children and, after they fell asleep, we would kiss, hug, and grope long into the evening. Another girl I met later was a blonde who lived in West Buffalo and her kissing lessons were really wild and I was crazy about her for months. Her mother liked me and she would find ways to make sure the girl and I were together often. Her grandmother liked me, but she counseled me to avoid her granddaughter, because she was a troubled teenager and wrong for me. I'm not sure what caused her grandmother to sense that about me, but I'm sure glad she advised me that way. I could sense a wild attitude in the girl that felt wrong and in short order I broke up with her, and felt much better as a result.

Thus our High School years ended. Our mentors Fliss and Ductor did a good job in instilling a good work ethic and a desire to do our best at whatever we tackled in life. I thanked them many times over, and as Mr. Ductor would say "[W]e didn't teach you fellows so much, as pointed you in the right direction. How far you got on the path, was up to you." How true, how true.

Often the focal point of high school commencement addresses, the end of high school symbolizes the beginning of a new chapter in one's life. So it was with Frank, who, after a few years of helping his father with the home finances, persuaded the elder Szachta to allow Frank to continue on with the post-graduate CAA A&E Licensing course. Frank eventually passed the written and practical portions of his Engine (power plant) exam, and the written portion of the airframe exam, but the school year ended before Frank could pass his airframe practical. Nevertheless, the training and certification assisted him in landing a job with the Twin Coach company.

The Twin Coach company was formed in 1927 by brothers Frank and William Fageol, who splintered off from another company with ideas to revolutionize the bus manufacturing world. They believed the frame and body could be unified into a single structure, and that the busses would perform better with two "twin" engines. Their idea became a success, but bus manufacturing began to wane with the increased popularity of individual automobile ownership. Not to worry, the plant's Buffalo location once again proved to be a godsend, attracting the likes of Boeing, Bell Helicopter, and the Grumman Aircraft companies, who sub-contracted with Twin Coach to manufacture aircraft and their parts.

Upon graduation from his post-graduate education, Frank landed a job with Twin Coach, building airplane parts for Grumman. All was going swimmingly for Frank—

and his friend Len Strzelec, a classmate and friend who joined Twin Coach with Frank—until January of 1951.

While at Twin Coach, Frank learned a lesson about workplace politics that resonated in him for many years after.

We were put to work on the swing shift 4pm till midnight at the airplane factory. We were building wings and ailerons as a subcontractor for the Grumman Company of Long Island, New York. We built these wings for a large single engine sub-hunter plane. My job involved the ailerons[5] of these wings. The plane was so big, that these ailerons were almost as big as the wings of the small Piper I flew! As we worked there about a year and a half, the schedule sped up as the Korean war was getting closer, and the "Cold War" was heating up. There were many weeks we worked a 12 hour shift for weeks at a time, to meet the delivery schedule. This was grueling, to say the least and we welcomed the return to a 40 hour week every time it returned.

My friend Len Strzelec and I were PG students together, and we both worked at the plant. I rode in a car pool with a neighbor, and paid him for the rides to and from work. As November 1950 rolled around our small aileron crew lost our "lead Man" due to a work speed up and the next man on the seniority list was an older Polish man (like myself) who had trouble communicating well in English.

---

[5] a hinged surface in the trailing edge of an airplane wing, used to control the airplanes' roll axis.

He suggested to me that I should take the Lead Man slot, and I agreed it was the logical thing to do.

What I didn't know was that my upper level foreman and the plant leaders had agreed that I would not get this promotion due to my being of draft age. With the Korean War coming, they figured I would be drafted soon, and they'd need another Lead Man. I felt that this was against the law, and I was furious that they would go through with this deal. They stuck together against me, and I was really mad as my union boss prevailed against one of his union brothers. Len Strzelec and I decided "we would show these guys." The Korean war was escalating since the Chinese Communists were testing President Truman's Containment Policy. The United Nations troops under General Macarthur's leadership was stopping the communists at Korea's 38th parallel. Things were heating up, and Len and I decided that if we were going to avoid becoming foot soldiers we better enlist. So, on January 4, 1951, Len and I joined the U.S. Air Force where, we believed, our love of aviation and airplanes would best suit us.

At the tender age of 21, Frank had already enjoyed a full and fruitful life, and times in high school are fondly remembered due in large part to his camaraderie with his mentors, Fliss and Ductor. He stayed in touch with both over the years, until their deaths. Friends always.

CHAPTER FOUR:

OFF WE GO

Air Force Basic Military Training, called BMT by the Air Force (presumably long before Subway restaurants invented the (B)iggest, (M)eatiest, (T)astiest sandwich), is similar to basic training in the other military branches and includes courses in basic war skills, military discipline, physical fitness, drill and ceremonies, Air Force core values and a comprehensive range of subjects relating to Air Force life. The training typically lasts approximately eight weeks, and is mean to indoctrinate trainees by making a smooth transition from civilian to military life.

Although the vast majority of 1950's recruits attended BMT at Lackland, the Air Force also had a small training base in New York. Common sense might dictate that enlistees from New York would attend BMT at a location requiring the least amount of travel. The military, however, isn't always interested in common sense. Frank

----

headed out to Texas.

After we enlisted at the Air Force recruiting station downtown, we were sent for a strip down physical in a large group of men, all enlisting at the same time. After we passed the physical, we were sworn in as US Air Force enlisted men, and swore allegiance to defend and protect our nation and its laws. There was a new USAF Basic Training Base being started at Sampson AFB, in lower NY' State, and of course the major Basic Training Base at Lackland AFB, San Antonio, Texas. Our whole group was ordered to Lackland, and a few days later we boarded a long troop train at the New Central Train Station in East Buffalo. This was the same railroad company that Pa worked for.

Lackland Air Force Base in San Antonio, Texas, is aptly called the, "Gateway to the Air Force." Since 1946, Lackland has been the basic training home to more than 7 million recruits. In 1950, as a response to the Korean Conflict, the Air Force announced a policy of "unlimited recruiting," which opened the doors for a lot of young men who were facing the draft. By the middle of January, 1951, Lackland was home to 55,000 trainees—on a base with a capacity of 25,000. Summarily, the Air Force suspended enlistments.

But the overcrowding, caused by the surge in recruitment, had some very real logistical fallout.

Our first impression of Lackland was its huge size. The base was full of blocks and blocks of two story barracks that stretched for miles in all directions. What really surprised us was the final mile of the trip, when we entered a site that was full of Army khaki brown tents. This was known as "tent city" and this was to be our home for Basic Training. Of course we were disappointed, since we expected to stay in the barracks we saw as we drove into the base. Although the warm weather felt nice, we were told that it does freeze here sometimes, and the tents sure wouldn't keep you warm in such conditions. Len Strzelec and I were assigned to our tent, and we picked canvas cots next to each other. We were started in training for drill and marching turns, even while we still were in our civilian clothes. We soon learned that the build-up for the Korean War was going on at a massive scale, and the base couldn't handle all the logistics needed to move our training along. The first order of business was the issue of military uniforms. The first items we were issued were boots and long john underwear. We thought that was a funny order of things, but a few cool nights in a row, taught us that the long john underwear felt good. One of the first pictures we took was of all of us near our tent in our Khaki long john underwear. After about a week, it turned cold. and moisture and snow hit our tents during the night, and we had to beat the tents with sticks to knock the ice off the tents and tent support ropes, so they would not collapse. It was bone chilling cold, since our clothing issue was moving very slowly.

One element of BMT is to assess the skills, abilities and potential of each recruit. Matching a recruit with a career in the Air Force with that recruit's capabilities and,

----

to some degree, his or her desires, is one goal of training
assessment. This is accomplished via a series of tests.
Naturally, the ever-thinking Frank had a plan.

During this period we were started on a testing series
called the "stanine" tests. They covered every job aspect of
Air Force duty, and the top score in any zone was a nine.
We discussed among ourselves our tactics in taking these
tests. None of us liked or wanted to be relegated to clerical
duties, so we were determined to try and do poorly on tests
in these fields. Of course, mechanic, math and science tests
were up our alley, and we tried to do our best on these tests.
The tests were graded on a scale of 1-9. After the test results
started to return, we were happy to see that our plan worked
well. Len Strzelec and I received "nines" on every test-
except the clerical duty tests, where we got 5's and 6's!

After these evaluations, which were done in the first
two weeks of BMT, training proceeded on an expedited
schedule. The Korean War was heating up, while the Texas
January was anything but. Rumors floated around the base
of recruits freezing to death due to the lack of adequate
uniforms, but those rumors appear to be false. Living in
tents in the winter, even in Texas, is, at the very least, an
unpleasant experience. At least it wouldn't be too long.

The cold and icy nights were rough, and rumors
started to the effect that several basic trainees died during
the cold spell. One rumor even had one trainee committing
suicide. We found out later that these were rumors only, but

the tension among the troops was high.

The big shocker came soon. Due to the crowded conditions, the Air Force was going to assign us to our next base at the one month time-line. We expected Basic to be about 8 weeks long. The need for troops at the schools and bases was the big driver that accelerated our rapid departure.

The next "shocker" is yet another example of fate playing its hand, and occurred as a direct result of Frank's intentional sand-bagging on the assessment evaluations.

The second big surprise came next. Instead of Len and I being assigned to aircraft mechanic duties, I was assigned to attend Airborne Radio Mechanic School at Scott AFB, Illinois, just East of St. Louis, while Len was assigned to Radar Mechanic School at Keesler AFB, near Biloxi, Mississippi. It turned out that our high "stanine" grades placed us into the training pools for electronics, which were critically short of students at this time.

As the 4 week time passed after our entry into Basic Training, we were loaded on trains again to travel to our next USAF assignment. It was now early Feb 1951, and in our fancy Air Force uniforms, we were on our way into our military career.

Scott Air Force Base is situated in St. Claire County, near Belleville, Illinois, a mere 20 miles from St. Louis. Frank had spent a brief amount of time in St. Louis before, when the train from Buffalo to Lackland for BMT training

----

made a rest stop at Union Station.

The train was all coach cars (no sleepers), and every seat was full. The train would chug along for 4 to 5 hours, and then stop at a small town where vendors would board the train with soda, coffee, sandwiches, and other snacks. We were given a few dollars ration allowance each day, and we would chow down on all kinds of snacks at each stop. Some of the stops were to let other trains pass, and we would sit in one siding for a hour or so, with no idea for the reason or duration of the stop. When we were about half way to Texas, after running along all through the night, we pulled into Union Station in St. Louis, Missouri. We were told that this was a 4-hour stop, that we could leave the train, but not to wander too far since we were to move out again in 4 hours.

We wandered into Union Station and were amazed at its huge size There were about 40 sets of rails backing trains into this huge open ended shed that then opened into a huge concourse, with a hotel and restaurant, barber shop, and more. Little did I realize that my future wife may have been working at the soda fountain the very day we were there. Coincidentally, her father was a barber in the barber shop in Union Station too, probably on duty at that very moment!

Len and I left Union Station and started to walk several blocks north and south of the station. Since we didn't know the layout of the streets as they related to downtown, we were afraid to get too far from the train station. After a couple of hours, and a small lunch at a corner restaurant near the rail station, we headed back to our train. All in all, I guess we spent about 5 hours in St. Louis on our way to Texas.

And now, as fate would have it, Frank was returning to the St. Louis area. Airborne Radio Mechanic School at Scott AFB had been training both operators and mechanics for several decades, but, after a systematic evaluation prior to the Korean War, it was found to be overemphasizing theory while being short on "hand-on" training. During the Korean Conflict, the Communications School at Scott Air Force Base revised its courses to meet wartime demands and to counter criticism that Scott radio mechanic graduates were overly trained in theory. On 19 July 1950, the school implemented a six-day academic week and divided the classes into shifts. Beginning in September 1950, the school changed its instructional method from the long-standing emphasis on theory to a more practical method of training in which students handled equipment and began to build a simple radio set on their first day of class. Students now gained a rudimentary understanding of radio theory by working with the equipment. Communications officer and cryptographic operator training remained part of the school's curriculum. Although the length of the courses varied, they were considerably shorter than the all encompassing radio course offered during World War II. In July 1952, at the height of the school's Korean War activities, over 6,000 communications students were in training at Scott AFB. This number dropped to 3,054 by year's end.[6]

The intense, six-day training week left Frank with pent up stress that he sought to offload on the weekends. And Frank loved to dance!

[6] Scott, Betty R., "An Illustrated History of Scott Air Force Base, 1917-1987, WorldCat Press, www.worldcat.org

---

Chapter Five: Love At First Sight

"Well our fathers fought the Second World War
Spent the weekend at the Jersey Shore
Met our mothers at the USO, asked them to dance,
Danced with them slow..."
--From "Allentown," by Billy Joel

After completing US Air Force basic training I was assigned to the Air Training Command's Airborne Radio Mechanic School at Scott AFB, in Illinois. My buddy Len Strzelec was at basic training with me, and he was assigned to attend Radar Mechanic School at Keesler AFB, near Biloxi, Mississippi. Scott AFB is located just 20 miles East of St. Louis, Missouri. I soon learned that hitch hiking this distance, especially in uniform, was easy to do. I arrived at Scott in early February 1951 and it sure was a cold month.

The old WWII barracks we moved into were a welcome change from the Tent City we lived in for basic

---

training at Lackland AFB, TX. We had a hard time learning how to fire up the coal furnaces in the barracks. We enjoyed the warmth but our inexperience led to many smoky nights as we tried to learn the secrets of furnace stoking and proper damper operation.

Frank Szachta, always learning.

The Airborne Radio Mechanic School was an interesting adventure. The military schools were run on six-hour shifts and my first series of classes were from 6AM till noon, six days a week. The mess hall food was bland (especially to my buddies) but filling and hot, and it tasted really good to me. Many of my classmates had mothers that were good cooks and these guys often complained about the mess hall meals. Since us kids at home cooked most of our meals since Ma died (along with Pa's cooking), the mess hall meals were different each day and they really tasted great to me.

Our classes included lessons in the Morse code with its entire dot and dash letters. The Air Force had a neat way for us to learn the letters. It consisted of listening to the dot and dash combinations for each letter and instead hearing a series of words that the dots and dashes sounded like. In no time at all most of us succeeded in passing the test for up to 13 words per minute in Morse Code sending and receiving, just the speed needed to finish that part of our training.

Frank performed well enough in technical school that he was in the ten percent of his class who were ordered to remain at Scott for advanced training. There was an interval of about a month between the end of basic school and the commencement of advanced training, which proved to be a fun-filled and perhaps fateful four weeks.

The school was over by mid-1951. The time seemed to zip by. I did well in the school and ranked near the top of my class, boy was I proud. The Air Force was expanding so fast, that they had trouble filling the classes the advanced training at the technician level during this phase of the Korean war build-up. Thus, they took the top 10% of our graduating class and assigned us to the technician level advanced school. During the month waiting period for our advanced school to commence we were given the "casual duty" job of painting barracks, all over the base. It was a big joke that the Base Commanders wife loved pastel colors, since the paint we used was tan, pink and soft yellow, and other such non-military colors. It was an enjoyable job to me since I always liked to paint, since I was a teen-ager. It seemed to me that your progress was easy to measure and this made it a satisfying task for me. Of course there was no homework assignment so typical during class work, that made this an easy job also. Since there was no homework, we had more time for social activities with my buddies. One of the service clubs hired a sergeant and his wife to teach us young GI's how to dance. Since they were both former Arthur Murray instructors, their lessons were a lot of fun and easy to follow. My grade school drum playing came in handy too, since I easily saw the beat and rhythm in all the songs and dances. The weird part of these lessons was that we danced with our buddies. My partner usually was a classmate named Jerry Scarpino. He was shorter than I was but he weighed 220 pounds. We looked quite the pair, especially when jitterbug lessons started.

Once I learned most of the dance steps for Fox Trot, Jitterbug, Waltz, Rumba, and Polka I was ready to try my luck by going to a dance with girls. The Base Service Clubs and those in nearby St. Louis sponsored weekly dances. These dances became more and more fun. My confidence level on the dance floor was soaring. It seems the drum playing I did in the PS #44 Band had provided me with rhythm that made dancing easy to learn, and my improvement grew by leaps and bounds.

The advanced school started in August of 1951 and our dances were trimmed as school with its homework assignments started again. We usually pushed the study time hard so that we could still make a week night dance at the Base Gym and a Saturday night dance at the top floor of the YWCA in downtown St. Louis. By then I had become a close buddy with a classmate named Al Maino from Philadelphia, PA. We usually hitchhiked a ride to St. Louis for these Saturday night dances. About the 15th of September 1951 we were at the YWCA dance in St. Louis

---

and we spotted two good-looking girls…

Nedra remembers:
One night, Jane and I were
Standing together and this guy was
Dancing by himself, surrounded
By some other fellows.
Suddenly, he was coming our way!
Oh my gosh!

Frank says:
My choice was a slender girl about my height
while Al's was a buxom girl that matched Al's 5ft 8 1nch
size.
I asked mine for a dance…
She said her name was Nedra, and I told her that it was
unusual
and she told me her mother read it
in a book and liked its sound.
Nedra was a great dancer and
I really liked dancing with her and doing
the steps our Sergeant instructor taught us.
We especially had fun learning the various
jump and twirl steps of the Jitterbug.

He taught me to do the Jitterbug…
and we've been dancing together ever since…

Call it what you will—fate, the universe, the cosmos, or God—but Frank and Nedra were destined to meet. For reasons unknown, St. Louis called to Frank, and attached itself to a place in his being. When he and Nedra finally met, it all made sense. Frank was a low-rated enlisted man and Nedra was a high school graduate with a nice government job. The attraction to one another was immediate and strong, and they had their whole lives ahead of them. What could possibly go wrong?

We took the girls home that night by streetcar and were pleasantly surprised at how friendly they both seemed. I've always enjoyed writing notes and small letters and I started a letter writing campaign to Nedra between the weekly dances. It seemed like "love at first sight" to me and I was always anxious for the next Saturday's dance. Nedra and I were getting quite serious, but a glitch soon cropped up. A Polish girl I danced with at a previous base gym dance was at the Halloween dance, and so was Nedra. I felt I should dance with the other girl at least once so I made an excuse of going to the bathroom so I could leave Nedra for a few minutes. Nedra caught on and saw me dance with the other girl. She told her girlfriend Jane Eckles that we were through. The girls went home after the dance, and I knew I was in the doghouse.

Frank had enjoyed being a young man in the big city, no doubt about it. Dancing with and necking with a lot of girls was only natural for a young man in the fifties. But Frank realized that he'd made a colossal blunder that Halloween, and quickly set about with damage control.

I'm not sure exactly how or why, but I knew that I needed to get serious with Nedra and stop dancing and chasing other girls. My life felt like I was on a treadmill. Nedra and I seemed to be attracted to each other like metal filings to a magnet and it felt so right, that I knew I must pursue her and capture her for my own as soon as possible.

Happily for me, after the Base Halloween dance fiasco, our coming together again was rapid and final. I never danced with another girl again after our patch-up weeks later. We soon started to have our own favorite songs and one of them is "Unforgettable" by Nat King Cole. His soft voice and nice melodies were very danceable, and his lyrics fit our loving feelings toward each other to a T.

By November of 1951 we were going steady. Without asking her to marry me, the conversation just seemed to gravitate to engaged or married couple conversations. We talked of 'what kind of car do we want to buy?' 'How do you think we can get married with a likely Korean assignment coming up in May 1952?' I asked her "How would you like to come visit my family in Buffalo when we get Christmas leave from school?" Well, all these conversations, dances, kisses, and hugs led to a lot of answers. At first, my East Buffalo accent seemed harsh and tough to Nedra. But, I had a real strong ally in Nedra's mother, Wannie Kimberlin. I'm not sure why she liked me or thought I might make a good husband for her daughter, but she did. I learned in later years, that Wannie was an excellent person that had a unique talent for foreseeing the future. I learned even later that Nedra inherited this talent as well. So, one by one, the answers started flowing. "Yes," Nedra said she would visit my family in Buffalo in December.

Meeting the family of one's significant other for the first time is nerve-wracking. First of all, Nedra was a WASP (White Anglo-Saxon Protestant) from Missouri heading up to meet the heavily Roman Catholic, proudly Polish family of her beloved Frank. The Szachtas had spoken both English and Polish in the household until Frank was ten; Frank's mother felt strongly about keeping their Polish roots alive. The cuisine at home maintained that tradition as well, as much as the family budget—and the creative culinary skills of Winnie and Eileen—could, anyway. Pa did a little cooking, too. The trip to Buffalo that December was interesting, to say the least.

The Buffalo visit had its high and low points. Nedra almost got ill after trying Pa's Duck soup. It's very tart and greasy soup made from the ducks blood. The taste nearly got Nedra, and the explanation of the ducks blood in the soup finished her off. She still claims to this day that my father didn't like her because of her "soup episode" even though I've told her over and over that it isn't so. Fact is, all my family became very fond of Nedra almost immediately, including Pa. Of course the soup was a low point in her visit. Our visit and photos of Niagara Falls were priceless. The icicles were two and three feet long and beautiful. This was a very high point of the visit.

Nedra had to stay at a downtown hotel since our home on Koons Avenue was too small for a guest to stay. So, each night we would return to her hotel on the streetcar and enjoy a hot chocolate at the Deco restaurant in her hotel. They were warm and sweet on those cold December nights. What more could two lovers want? We heard later that our late night farewells caused rumors about our pre-marital activities. These rumors would be fueled even more in the following months when Nedra and I decided to advance our wedding date so that we could get to know each other before I would be sent to Korea. But, we kept our physical time together to kissing and snuggling.

Later, Nedra agreed, "Yes, let's get married in May when you finish your school" at Scott. My Lt. Squadron Commander finally allowed our plans for marriage to proceed since I was positive that we would make a success of this marriage.

Nedra started to take Roman Catholic instructions since it was clear to both of us that the church's position on marriage "till death do us part" was a great way to start our married life together.

Upon returning to St. Louis, Nedra continued in her job as a GS-3 civil servant at the Army Records Center. I returned to school at Scott and we started making wedding plans. Nedra's father was a barber at Union Railroad Station in St. Louis. He did very well during the Korean War since servicemen passed through Union Station by the thousands. Most of them wanted a shoeshine, haircut and shave during their stop there. Nedra and I found a clean 1942 dark green 4-door Plymouth car at a dealer near their home. Nedra's father said he would be glad to co-sign the car loan even though he never owned a car himself. The Plymouth cost $360, and we would pay it off in one year with monthly payments of $39. Nedra accelerated her Catholic lessons and we set a new wedding date of Feb 23, 1952. This was a Saturday and the Lt. Commander agreed to give me and Al Maino as my best man the day off school for the wedding. Our honeymoon would be Sunday since school resumed at 6AM on Monday.

The wedding took place at 9AM on a Saturday at St. Margaret's church about six blocks from Nedra's home at 2606 Louisiana St. in south St. Louis. Al was the Best Man and Jane Eckols, Nedra's friend and Al's girl friend at the dances' was her Bridesmaid. Nedra wore a lovely Navy Blue suit and Jane wore a pretty Bridesmaid dress. Al and I wore the USAF Dress Blue uniform with white shirts and a black bow tie. We were two spiffy couples. A big surprise appeared at the wedding and reception when two friends from Buffalo, Len Strzelec and Joe Schiersing drove into town in an old jalopy. It was a very nice surprise. The wedding reception was held at Nedra's parent's home, which we had cleaned and painted for the occasion. Remember I told you I liked to paint.

The big one-day honeymoon was spent at a motel near Belleville, Illinois. We were exhausted from the wedding day, and reception, and most of all from the wild assortment of drinks we tried during the wedding day.

Since we were novices at drinking we had such crazy drinks as scotch and sweet soda, wines, and other nondescript concoctions. With all these weird drinks, and the rush of the home painting and more, Nedra got ill on Sunday with flu and nausea. We returned to her home early on Sunday night and got razzed by her parents and brothers Bill and Jerry because we bought the big Sunday edition of the St. Louis Post Dispatch newspaper on our honeymoon day, but never opened it.

Six months after that magical night on the dance floor at the YWCA, Frank and Nedra were married. Says Nedra, "It was forty years ago—thinking back, it doesn't seem that long ago! The night I met Frank was the luckiest night of my life—he is the BEST!"

With little income, the new couple lived with Nedra's family in the apartment in St. Louis. Frank left early each

----

day and drove the Plymouth—the "Green Hornet"—to Scott and back, working his way through advanced school and wondering if he was headed to Korea.

I've often said the "God takes care of fools and angels" and I am not sure which category I fit into. Instead of getting a Korean assignment I was sent to Bryan AFB, Texas, a Pilot Training Base. I was to be an Airborne Radio Technician in the field radio repair shop; A great assignment. Now maybe we could find the time for a real honeymoon.

My school graduation came, and since I was near the top of the class again, I was awarded a promotion to Corporal, a two-striper. So in a few days, we packed our life possessions into the back seat of our 42 Plymouth and drove to Texas as Corporal and Mrs. Frank Szachta. Boy, were we proud of our progress and I most of all for the blessing and good fortune of meeting and marrying Nedra, the apple of my eye.

CHAPTER SIX: NEW AIRMAN, NEW HUSBAND, NEW LIFE

Although Bryan Air Force Base (formerly Bryan Army Air Field, or AAF) had been closed in 1947, the build-up for the Korean War forced the Air Force to exercise its right of recapture, and in the spring of 1951, purchased most of it back and reopened as Bryan Air Force Base, under the Air Training Command. The base, situated approximately 75 miles northwest of Houston, was utilized as a pilot training facility, instrument instructor training facility, and the supporting infrastructure for that mission. In fact, astronaut Virgil "Gus" Grissom—one of the original Freedom Seven astronauts who later lost his life in the launch pad fire on Apollo 1—was a flight instructor at Bryan in the 1950's. In 1961, the land and buildings were

----

deeded to the Agricultural and Mechanical College of Texas, now Texas A&M.[7]

In order to fully understand the Szachta's life, one must embrace the family dynamic that existed in mid-Twentieth Century America. Books, movies, television shows, etc., exist that give us a look into the "American way of life" during the period, and we can all accept that some poetic license had been taken by those who faithfully went about telling the story of the lives and times in a nation unknowingly prepping itself for major change. The majority of that century found the United States either in or on the head- or tail-end of war. The American People, God-fearing and patriotic, were amassed as one in the battle for "Freedom;" first in Europe, then the South Pacific and, again, Europe. The government and the media were able to rally America's citizenry, with the perceived fear of socialism and communism as the standard. In time of war and/or political unrest, a nation—a community, a family—tends to adjust battle lines, while, in times of prosperity and peace, those lines turn inward. Think of it this way: When siblings live in security and safety, they establish a pecking order in the family. They engage in rivalry that simmers and can even rise to the physical. However, when an outsider threatens any family member, the balance of the siblings unify against the outside threat. It's the same with countries.

---

[7] Texas Historical Society, http://www.tshaonline.org/handbook/online/articles/qbb06

In the mid-Nineteenth Century, the United States was engaged in a brutal war within its own borders. Lines of demarcation were established and countrymen took up arms against their own; even brothers fought on opposite sides. By the turn of the century, the nation had begun to heal, the economy was recovering nicely, and governmental leadership engaged the counsel of business tycoons to continue to build and strengthen America. When the call came to join up with allies against a common enemy who threatened those allies' "freedom," the United States gathered her resources and joined in the fight. World War I, and especially World War II, required the American People to sacrifice, to ignore any remnants of civil angst, and to unify according to the government's desires. In so doing, American families fell into a natural hierarchy within themselves. Put simply, men went to war, women stayed home. Men fought on the battlefront—no small task—and women were left behind to keep things together, both in the family and in society as a whole.

Considering the stories told of the earliest pioneers who set westward, this was not exactly a new development. History books are replete with stories of strong, brave women who held the homefront while their cowboy or soldier or miner husbands left the home to perform their duties to both family and nation. Women like Diana Lucina Block, Elizabeth Bradshaw, Naomi Hedges and Eunice Pratt—to name but a very few—blazed trails westward, often pushing carts or driving a team of mules; cooked, sewed, did laundry, birthed and raised children, not to mention often lending a hand on the ranch, in the family business or anywhere else they were needed.

With the entrance of the Industrial Revolution in the early Twentieth Century, the role of many men turned from agricultural entrepreneur to employee. Educated men acquired positions in business while those men who "got their hands dirty" for a living went to work building railroads, automobiles, drilling for oil and gas, harvesting timber and mining America's natural resources. Women— mothers—stayed at home providing support for their husbands, raised the family and kept house. The Feminist Movement of the late Twentieth Century—a bold and worthy endeavor, the goal of which was to extend the invisible barriers and boundaries which prevented women from embarking into traditional male occupations and education—criticized mothers and grandmothers for "accepting" their submissive role in the family. Ironically— some argued—the Feminist Movement, designed to raise America's consciousness to the voice of Woman, neglected to consider that a percentage of their own sought to exercise that right by enjoying more traditional roles within the family and society.

By the mid-Twentieth Century, America's prosperity translated into the so-called "Suburban Sprawl," in which the outlying areas surrounding larger metropolitan areas began to blossom with housing developments, commercial and industrial entities, schools and recreational centers. America's military—on standdown after the Second World

War victories—began to once again build against another threat: Global Thermonuclear War, referred to as the "Cold War." Additionally, the threat of communism in, primarily, Asia, still held the attention of America's armed forces. Men were being called into action for the Korean Conflict and, ultimately, the "Police Action" in Viet Nam. In other words, war still draped herself over the American landscape like a giant, ill-defined cloud.

Why all of this is important to the Szachta's story should be evident, but let's clarify. Nedra Szachta had the heart of a pioneering woman who loved her life. She loved her husband unconditionally, and would not have traded places with anyone. Taking care of her household, her children, and supporting Frank in each of his endeavors was always the desire of her heart.

Nedra writes:

We were married February 23, 1952. I was barely 19 and he was 21 and a half. We bought a 10-year old car (my father co-signed the $350 loan) and we made car payments for a year. We lived with my parents from February to May. We feared [Frank] would be deployed to Korea but we were sent *together* to Bryan, Texas. He was corporal (2-stripes) when we were married so money was tight but we were never broke. We always had a little savings. I guess our poor childhoods taught us something! I have not worked outside the house since we left for Texas, where our first son, Stephen, was born on July 22, 1953.

Poor Frank! I think I must have sent him to the drugstore five times that first day home from the hospital! If Dr. Spock said you needed this—then we needed it. Quite an experience—800 miles from my mother and a new baby!! At least when you buy a new lawn mower you get a detailed instruction book! We all managed to survive, but that first baby was really a Guinea Pig! Today, he's a high school math and computer teacher, and head track coach at Hazelwood Central [Missouri] High School.

Frank writes:

Our first assignment after getting married was as an Airborne Radio Technician, with Air Force Specialty Code (AFSC) 30171. I found out after arrival at Bryan AFB as a Corporal (2-stripe enlisted man) that the 30171 code was for Staff Sergeants and above. By going through the advanced school right after the mechanic level school, I had leap-frogged ahead. A few months later, the higher level NCO's at the base had my work code lowered to 30151, due to my lower rank. I was one of the few "5-level" electronic types to achieve my code from above.

The warrant Officer in charge of our field maintenance Radio Repair shop gave me heavy responsibilities at once. One of my first repair jobs involved rewiring an AT-6 training plane completely. I learned all about aircraft electronic wiring harnesses in a hurry. Several of the radio shop civilian employees helped us younger airmen learn our duties quickly.

By now Nedra was pregnant with our first child. Since we only had a dispensary on the base, the childbirth would take place in the town hospital. Coincidentally our friends the Descamps were to deliver their first child a week before ours. When the due date arrived, I took Nedra to the hospital early one morning. Linda had gone in a few days before. As Nedra neared the end of labor, I heard that Linda was having a hemorrhage and needed some blood. I had been a blood donor for a while by then and volunteered to give blood for Linda's needs. Because I was a serviceman, I could only give blood at the base dispensary, and I had to drive from the hospital to the base for the blood donation. After I gave blood, the "Green Hornet" wouldn't start up for my return trip to town. Finally someone gave me a jump-start, and I quickly drove back to the hospital. As I ran to the second floor, I saw Nedra's room was empty, as well as the delivery room also. I rushed all over asking if Nedra was OK, and was it a boy or a girl?

Finally a nurse took me to Nedra's new room, and told me that she was fine and so was our newborn boy. She didn't realize I had been gone during the delivery to donate blood for Linda's needs. Both mothers recovered well, and soon were at home on Nall Lane tending their babies.

We lived in Bryan, a small east Texas town with a population of about 4000. We found a nice small rental apartment where a widow had split up her several cottages into small apartments. We were on the second floor of one cottage with a small kitchen, a tiny bedroom and a tinier bathroom. We were both learning our roles, as young married persons and Nedra's first big meal was a huge pot of spaghetti with meat sauce. She used a 16-ounce pack of spaghetti, not realizing how much pasta that makes. We ate spaghetti Monday, Tuesday, Wednesday, and Thursday. Since we Catholics don't eat meat on Fridays, we threw out the remaining sauce and pasta that night. It really was excellent spaghetti though, and I love her spaghetti to this day. In fact, I learned how she made it, and in later years I would become a good spaghetti cook myself.

After we were stationed at Bryan for nearly six months, we decided to take a short 3-day pass and take a second honeymoon to make up for the one day honeymoon that we had right after our wedding. We planned to drive about 130 miles south to Galveston Island on the Gulf of Mexico and get some sun tan in the process. We drove through the flats of southern Texas and got a nice motel right near the water. We didn't take any sun protection, and spent quite a bit of time on the rocks and beach to get some fast sun tan. Our big problem was that we were both very white from not being out in the sun for a long time, and we did not realize how intense the Texas sun can be in mid-day. Our second night in the motel was quite painful, as we got burned badly, and looked like a couple of cooked lobsters. The last day there we spent with lotion and cool towels on our backs, to try and recover from the bad burn we got. Fortunately I tan easily, so my burn cooled quicker than

Nedra's, so I could resume work OK a day after we drove home from this honeymoon. It was an experience almost as rough as our first honeymoon, and we soon learned that just being together and enjoying married life can be one enjoyable and happy honeymoon.

In reality, Our two plus years at Bryan were the best honeymoon we could have ever have had. The small town life was a new and pleasant experience for both of us, and a splendid way to begin our married life together. It was a quiet town and our new Air Force and civilian friends were great. Our first Air Force tour was a super way to start a sterling Air Force career. We had help from many sources including our big boss, God. Our health, and our baby's health, this fine assignment, and our rapid enlisted promotions all displayed God's blessings on our family. We were and still are very grateful for these many blessings.

We made four very good friends from the base, in this small apartment complex. Art and Rita Burzynski were from Buffalo, NY my hometown. He was a Staff Sergeant and was friends for our entire tour at Bryan. We wrote them for years afterward, and stayed in touch till about 1960 or so, when they stopped vvriting us. The other couple we met was George and Linda DesCamp from Ft. Worth, Texas. Later in our tour at Bryan, we three couples ended up living in small apartments in a small house at 700 Nall Lane. The owner of this home planned to tear it down and build a large home on the corner lot. He rented us the three small apartments for $30/Month with utilities included. One by one, we three friends moved into this home, and the low rent helped us all save a few dollars on our low enlisted rank pay. Margaret Clooney made a song called "This Old House" at the time, and we all had a good laugh, since the lyrics fit 700 Nall Lane perfectly.

With the Korean War growing, the pilot training on our base was expanding. Soon I was designing and building a Mobile Radio Control Tower to be mounted atop a flatbed truck body. Several of the shop civilians helped me complete two of these truck mounted control towers to be used by the flight instructors to control the many T-33 aircraft in the traffic pattern on the airfield. My next assignment was to work as the second shift chief in the radio shop. This job gave Nedra a chance to join me at work, since I was alone in the shop almost all of the time. Since the shop was air conditioned, this was nice for Nedra during the hot summer nights. I recall one funny incident one night, which involved Nedra's voice.

I needed to check out all the radios in the two mobile control towers each night and that wasn't always easy to do, since the regular tower wasn't always manned to respond to my calls. So I taught Nedra some radio call terminology and we would check the radios as follows. I would be in Mobile #1 and Nedra would be in Mobile #2. I would call her as follows: "Mobile #2, this is Mobile #1, how do you read?" Nedra would answer "Mobile #1, I read you loud and clear." So my work would go faster and Nedra could enjoy the coolness of the radio shop the rest of the evening. Remember that at that time there were very few females serving on active duty in the Air Force. Well, the regular control tower was open late one night for night flying, and they challenged the female voice. It took me a few minutes to explain myself to the regular control tower operators, and Nedra and I had some laughs over the incident.

During time of war, those in uniform often enjoy rapid advancement, especially when he or she serves with honor, commitment and enthusiasm. Frank was a hard-working, bright and energetic Airman, who regularly went above and beyond the call of duty. His performance captured the attention of his superiors, and in just over two years he had been promoted to the rank of Staff Sergeant. Frank took stock of where he was—and where he wanted to be.

Due to war pressures, promotions came often at each six-month point. Since our Radio Shop Chief, Johnny the Warrant Officer, kept giving me added responsibilities all the time, my rise to Staff Sergeant came after only 25 months in the service. Since there were no enlisted "super grades" above Master Sergeant at this time I could look forward to only two more promotions in the future. Nedra and I talked it over and decided to try the test for the Air Force Officer Candidate School (OCS).

There was a time in the military when enlisted men (and women, presumably) could sit for a test to determine if he or she were of officer material. The military, quite rightfully, determined that it was foolish not to consider those already a part of the service for the officer corps. Enlisted persons who scored well enough on the exams were sent to Officer Candidate School (OCS), a rigorous, intensely physical and mental six-months of training. Successful graduates were then commissioned as officers.

Since then, all the military branches suspended this practice, opting instead to recruit officers a) Right out of High School for appointments to the various military academies, or b) From the ranks of college graduates who had an interest in a military officer career. These latter often choose a college curriculum that includes courses offered in the Reserve Officer Training Corps (ROTC), and are still required to complete OCS.

Frank and Nedra's decision to try to gain acceptance into OCS was a wise one, but it would require him to dig deep within himself if he were to succeed.

By now I was the Non-Commissioned Officer In Charge (NCOIC) of the radio shop. A Captain replaced our Chief Warrant Officer, Johnnie. He cautioned me about the OCS and the risky nature of being a "Reserve" Officer for 16 years into the future. He counseled me to try and make the "Regular" Officer status as soon as possible, since a Reduction in Force (RIF) was always a threat to the Reserve Officers between war periods. This would cut your career short of the retirement point.

Nevertheless, in April of 1954 Frank sat for the OCS exam, and his grade on that exam was the highest ever recorded at Bryan AFB.

It's interesting to note that Nedra, in her writings, has little to say regarding role in convincing Frank to stay at OCS when he wanted to throw in the towel. That is classic Nedra; deflecting attention from herself. Nevertheless, as Frank tells his story, once Nedra came into his life, he immediately drops the pronoun "I" in favor of the pronoun "We." Frank and Nedra were two souls united as one, albeit with strong, independent and individual personalities. Frank was gifted with a brilliant, analytical mind that could scarcely comprehend the word "can't." Nedra, also highly intellectual but with a fanciful zest for life, endeared herself to anyone she met. Strong-willed but lovingly understanding, Nedra with her "contagious laughter" exemplified the law of attraction, drawing people into her realm by virtue of the joyful manner in which she traveled her journey. Together they formed a union that could best be described as formidable, with Nedra unabashedly leading the way.

For the first several weeks of OCS training, candidates are essentially segregated from any family. The rigors of making the transition into the officer ranks—physically, mentally and emotionally—require acute focus with no personal interruptions. The separation, combined with the demands of OCS training, can have debilitating effects upon officer candidates.

I had heard some horror stories about OCS, and recalled that a Staff Sergeant on base at Bryan had been accepted to OCS a few weeks earlier. However, I was surprised to see him on base again one day. He told me that OCS was horrible for him with lots of hazing, and that he quit after only four weeks of the school. I didn't let that deter me, and my application was accepted and I was ready to go to OCS at Lackland AFB in San Antonio, Texas, OCS Class 54D. This class would start in June 1954 and graduate in December 1954 at Lackland AFB. We were told that we must separate for the start of OCS due to the rigors of underclass days. We planned that Nedra would go to her parent's new home, a fine apartment on Clara St. in St. Louis, MO. Our plan was for her to join me later in San Antonio. It turned out that the early weeks of hazing from the upper classmen was so severe that I called Nedra after only 4 days of school and told her I wanted to quit. She reminded me of our friend who had quit earlier in the year and how humiliating it would be to go back to Bryan AFB after a failure, what with the "Highest grade ever on the base" and all the fine send-offs we experienced. She convinced me that I was stronger than that and tough enough to make the grade. She told me of our successes so far in our married life, and our Air Force work to date, and I went back to my barracks energized, and ready to give the school another chance. Her strong reassurance was well worth it. I bucked down, and stayed the course. Her guidance at that point was the best medicine I would ever take, and the decision to complete that school and achieve the Commissioned ranks was a top hallmark of our Air Force career.

After a number of weeks, Nedra and Stephen made the trip from St. Louis to Texas to be near Frank, as he adjusted to the routine of OCS. The intensity of those first few weeks caused some changes in Frank, which Nedra was about to discover.

Work and studies stabilized a bit, and as I kept losing weight due to the training and stress regimen of OCS, time flew by. Soon, it was time for Nedra to come south. She convinced her mother Wannie and Aunt Billy to accompany her on her trip from St. Louis to San Antonio, with our firstborn son, Stephen. Our gray '51 Plymouth was running well, and they made the trip fine. When they arrived in Texas, she was parked near our barracks, and I went out to meet her for our first time to see each other in about 6 weeks. I had lost 28 pounds due to the OCS training, and as I squared my corners going to our car, she thought this was some tiny OCS Cadet coming to tell her when and where she would get to see her husband. Much to her shock, that tiny Cadet was me. We kissed of course, and made plans for her to visit the OCS Cadet Club that Friday night for a party.

We found a small 2 room flat to rent where she and Stephen could live as I finished OCS School. As I said, we would meet for a Friday night Cadet Club gets together and again Saturday afternoon after our mandatory Saturday AM parade. At this time we could be together overnight at our rental flat, and get back to the OCS barracks by early Sunday afternoon.

An upperclassman named Mr. Womack (All us were called Mr.) decided to haze me and make me very late for the first OCS party with my wife. He had me in a brace (at attention) along the upper-class hall in the OCS barracks for nearly an hour. I was very angry, and flushed after he grilled me with "memory work" for nearly an hour. I finally got to the club, but never forgot that treatment by my upper-classman.

Nedra writes:

In the Spring of 1954 Frank decided to try the test for Officer Candidate School, since, in the 23 months of service he was already a Staff Sergeant. He scored the highest of anyone ever to be tested on that base, so in June he went to San Antonio and I went home with our year-old son to my parents (the hottest summer on record there!). It was a six-month school and probably the toughest thing he's ever been through! When I joined him in San Antonio, I hardly recognized him—he had lost 28 pounds in six weeks! We only go to see each other from noon Saturday to 6 P.M.

Sunday. Plus, a dance on Friday, but he had to be back at the barracks by midnight! As a reward for surviving, he was commissioned as a Second Lieutenant and we joined the officer ranks!

OCS continued, with Frank, Nedra and Steve now living together in Texas. The remainder of the training was grueling for Frank, with advanced classes, more upper-class hazing, and emotionally-taxing physical training. OCS is intentionally difficult for the body, mind and spirit of the candidates. Many will go on to become pilots who must perform well under duress, but even those who don't must behave in exemplary manners when faced with any stressful situation. The phrase, "officer and a gentleman" is not taken lightly by those who rise to the level of military officer. The few moments of enjoyment with his family are recalled fondly, including dances at the OC club and weekends when he could semi-relax.

Our memories of these times were both good and bad. Bad in the memories of the upper-class hazing and hours separation from each other that such treatment generated. Good in the memories of our dances at the OC (Officer Candidate) dances we enjoyed each Friday evening. Also our Saturday afternoons and nights together were very, very good memories. One other bad memory was our graduation dance, the night before our Officer

Commissioning ceremony. The Base Officers Club was "Off-Limits" for our dance, since we were not officers yet. We knew of many ROTC and Academy events held in officers clubs, We were very upset that the Officers in charge saw fit to deny us the use of their Club, the night before we got our Commission. All in all, it was a tough school. That led to an exciting career in the USAF, and best of all helped us a achieve that 20-year retirement goal we set back in early 1954.

Frank was now a brand spanking new Second Lieutenant in the United States Air Force, a "shavetail," in military vernacular. The question now was, "Where will I go next?" Having a good deal of technical training and experience behind him as an enlisted man, the logical step would be moving forward in that direction. While logic is not high on the list of military decisions, this time the Air Force got it right. Frank was sent to Keesler Air Force Base in Biloxi, Mississippi.

In 1955, after graduating from OCS, we were sent to Communications/Electronics Office's school at Keesler Air Force Base. The technical side of this school was a breeze for me, since it was a repeat of many topics taught me during my schools in radio work at Scott AFB in 1951 and early 1952. Thus this school was almost like a vacation, since school sessions were only 6 hours per day. After the tough hours and athletics and hazing of the 6 months of OCS, this time was like a long honeymoon for Nedra and me and son Steve. The base Special Services had boats to rent and we took boat rides on the back bay behind the base several times. The Biloxi coast beaches were nice also, and swimming often was a relaxing pastime also.

Another fine aspect of our early days as a Lieutenant, we really enjoyed the fine Officers club on the base. They had excellent food at reasonable prices, and the "happy hour" with their cheap drinks, and especially the free shrimp *hors d'oeuvres*, were something we really enjoyed a lot. The Marine Room, with many tanks of tropical fish holds many fond memories of the good times we had there.

Keesler Air Force Base was initially opened in the summer of 1941 as an Aircraft Mechanics School. Later that summer, the base was named for 2d Lt Samuel Reeves Keesler, Jr., a Mississippi native and distinguished aerial observer, killed in action in France during the First World War. Keesler also operated for a time as a recruit training center. However, most of the commands based at Keesler were related to aircraft support training. Furthermore, Keesler is distinguished in American history because the Tuskegee Airmen[8] were trained there.

Frank and Nedra were happy to be amongst friends

---

[8] The Tuskegee Airmen were the first African-American military aviators in the United States armed forces. Battling—among many other obstacles—racial biases, the members of the "Red Tail" squadron served with honor and dignity, and distinguished themselves in numerous battles in WWII.

----

at Keesler.

We were blessed in other ways in that some of our OCS classmates were neighbors, and that was very nice. The Oryall family became very close friends. Orland was a high-ranking OCS Cadet Officer, and he and wife Betty and their children were Catholic like us, and were very friendly people. We became close friends here, and this friendship stayed warm throughout the years. Even now, we still write often, and plan to visit them again at their home in CA, near Vandenburg AFB in the near future.

Frank found a lot of the training to be a bit redundant; he'd had a good deal of technical training already as an enlisted man. In fact, one student in Frank's class was ultimately very happy to have Frank around.

There was a First Lieutenant in our class named Sam. He was a college graduate, and an ROTC Officer. Sam was pretty "loose" in his military bearing, compared to us OCS alumni. One cold day at Keesler, Sam came to class in his khaki's with a suede jacket to keep warm. Of course "we" all knew Sam was "out of uniform" in such attire, but his ROTC Training didn't teach him this detail, apparently. Our Class leader, a Major, told Sam "to get that jacket off, and never mix civvy clothing with his uniform again." That brought a chuckle to us "sharp" OC's. But there was another issue that arose that I remember Sam for. He was having trouble passing the technical parts of our classes. This fact surprised me, since he was a college grad. Our class leader knew my electronic background, and he asked me to tutor Sam in our off class hours. Of course I would do it; a young "shavetail Lieutenant" like me doesn't question a superior's requests. As the weeks rolled by, I helped Sam make the grades in school, and he made it through the course OK.

But Lieutenant Sam tried to return the favor.

During our many sessions together, Sam being a superior (1st Lt that is) would try to enlighten me on his "secret formula for success in the USAF". He said "to succeed in the USAF, you had better become an expert in the games of bridge and golf." It seemed to me a stupid way to look for success, and sadly I locked these statements into my brain as – "I will not play bridge or golf, and I will succeed." Sadly, I think in hindsight that golf would have been a fine sport, that I may have enjoyed. The little I saw of bridge, the card game, I never missed. In later years I played 9 holes of golf on a few occasions, and enjoyed it.

As the course work dragged on, Frank was glad to be an officer, glad to have Nedra and Steve with him, and was generally a satisfied, happy man looking forward to a long term career in the Air Force. Becoming a pilot never really entered his mind.

Since we pondered our next career step after OCS we never considered volunteering for pilot training since I had a childhood health issue burned into my brain that bleeding gums caused one to fail the flying school physical exam. I read as a youngster during WWII that since the B-17 bomber was unpressurized, that if a person ever had bleeding gums, it would disqualify you for flying. As a youngster in a big (10 kids) family that was poor (Pa was a railroad laborer), I had toothaches fairly often. Since fillings at the dentist were much more expensive that extractions of the bad tooth, I had 8 teeth pulled during my younger years. Of course, during the tooth pulling, the gums would bleed, and this memory kept me from applying for the flight training physical.

During this school, many classmates were pilots and navigators, and they knew of my solo of the J-3 Piper Cub when I was 16 years old. Thus they could not figure out why I didn't apply for flight school out of OCS. After I told them my tale of "'bleeding gums", they were sure I could pass the flight physical.

"Applying for Flight School" and "being accepted for flight school" soon became significantly different acts, as Frank was about to learn.

Thus after we were about half way through the School, I discussed my flight school desire with a Master Sergeant at the Wing Headquarters. He felt that my strong desire to fly overshadowed the Service needs for another Communications Officer, and he convinced me to apply for the USAF flight school. He took me, a new "shavetail Lt." (another name for OCS graduates) and pressed me to continue in the application process. After I applied, the form went through channels to the Group for approval and forwarding. The WAF (Woman in the Air Force) at Group called me in to review my pilot training application. She counseled me that Air Force Regulations required one to work for years in the Comm/Electronic field to "pay back the AF" for the schooling in this field. I visited my mentor, the MSgt at Wing and briefed him the WAF Officers story. He told me to go back to Group and tell her to disapprove my application and forward it to Wing Headquarters. He then told me that he would write a strong approval letter approving my application for forwarding to AF

Headquarters. He stated that Wing positions are highly regarded while group positions are much lesser ranked. Sure enough, months later this came to pass.

As my MSgt mentor told me, he wrote a fine recommendation letter about my pilot training application, and his boss the Wing Commander signed it. Shortly, I was taking the flight physical, and as my classmate pilots told me, I passed the physical with flying colors. We were now getting close to school graduation, and orders for our next assignment were coming out. We were graduating in Dec 55, so with travel and leave we would report to our next assignment in January. My assignment arrived, for a job as a Communications Officer at Thule AFB. *Greenland.* A colder place in Jan I couldn't think of. In a week, another TWX (Military telegram) came out saying that my Thule assignment was "frozen" pending a decision on my Pilot Training application. Another week later, and my Thule assignment was cancelled and I was assigned to Pilot Training Class 57F at Bartow AB, FL. What a lucky break! A sad retrospective to this came shortly as my Thule assignment was bounced to a next class and my friend Orland Oryall picked up that assignment. The Oryalls just had a new child, and this was a low blow for their family. It is remarkable to us that they stayed our friends through this ordeal, and through the years to the present time. This was an experience that sure showed us what true friendship is, in its many twists and turns of life.

Nedra remembers:

Our first assignment after OCS was Biloxi, Mississippi, where Frank went to more electronics training —a lot of review for him (for 11 months). The pilots in his class convinced him to try for pilot training, so in December, instead of going to Thule, Greenland, for a remote (unaccompanied) assignment, we were off to Bartow, Florida for pilot training. The bad thing about this was that the remote assignment in Greenland was bumped back to the class behind Frank, and our best friends were saddled with that assignment. That meant being separated for a year. We were godparents to their new baby at the time and even though they got that bad assignment, believe it or not, we are still friends!

CHAPTER SEVEN:
BACK IN THE AIR

In 1950, the U.S. Government exercised its reversal clause for the facility at Bartow Airport and again took over control of that facility. The Department of Defense concurrently called for bids from civilian contractors to man and operate a primary pilot training school for U.S. Air Force student pilots. Renamed Bartow Air Base, the installation served as a USAF primary flight training facility for the Air Training Command (ATC) from 1951 to 1960, during which time its 3303rd Pilot Training Group operated the T-6 Texan, T-34 Mentor and T-28 Trojan, training both commissioned USAF officers and USAF aviation cadets. More than 8,000 men graduated from primary flight training at Bartow AB before proceeding on to select air force bases for advanced training in aircraft such as the T-33 Shooting Star for jet pilots or the TB-25 and B-25 Mitchell for multiengine pilots. [9]

As we signed into Bartow Air Base, we found out that Civilian pilot training bases such as this were not really Air Force Bases. All Officer Pilot Trainees live in civilian homes "on the local economy" as it is called.

We found a nice two-bedroom home to rent in Winter Haven, Florida. It was close to Bartow Air Base and had the base recreation area close by on one of the many lakes around Winter Haven. Also our first training would be done in Super Cubs at Gilbert Field, an auxiliary field near Winter Haven. In fact in later years it became known as Winter Haven field. During our leave period before classes started, I learned that the recreation area near our home contained a fleet of small aluminum skiffs with 25hp outboard motors for water skiing. I started to learn water skiing at once, and got up on a pair of water skis on my second try. Slalom or single ski work was much harder, and after many near drowning tries, I finally learned that difficult lesson also. Pilot training went rapidly, and my solo

[9] http://www.aetc.af.mil/shared/media/document/AFD-070130-081.pdf

and early lessons in the Super Cub went very well, thanks to my solo and lessons when I was 16 years old. The Super Cub was a 115 horsepower version of the J-3 Cub I first flew at 15 years of age, which was powered by a 65 hp engine. Not all the students had prior experience as I did, and ground loops[10] were quite frequent in our training since the bigger engine added torque to the tail wheel factors this plane had. In fact, our class had the misfortune of being the only class in years to experience fatalities in Super Cub training.

The first fatal accident involved a student doing his first solo takeoff. As his instructor cleared him for solo and got out of the plane, another Cub ground looped on the runway. This type-landing incident occurs when the student does not control the rudder fast enough, and the tail swings around, and the pilot has to stop the plane rapidly, before a wing tip scrapes the runway. After such a ground loop, the pilot must shut down the engine, and get towed into the ramp tail first. The ignominy of this towing should embarrass the pilot sufficiently so that he won't do this again. Thus, for over 10 minutes as the plane gets towed in tail first, this first solo student is sitting alone in his plane, awaiting his first solo take-off. Coincidentally I was taxiing out for my third solo take-off at this time. On his first solo take-off roll, this student pulled up too steeply and stalled

---

[10] In aviation, a ground loop is a rapid rotation of a fixed-wing aircraft in the horizontal plane while on the ground. Aerodynamic forces may cause the advancing wing to rise, which may then cause the other wingtip to touch the ground. In severe cases (particularly if the ground surface is soft), the inside wing can dig in, causing the aircraft to swing violently or even cartwheel. Love, Michael Charles (1995). *Better Takeoffs & Landings*. McGraw-Hill Professional. pp. 75–76. ISBN 0-07-038805-9

the plane, and entered into a right turn spin. At such a low altitude, there was chance for him to pull out and recover, and he crashed right in front of me, about half way down the runway. He died on impact. It turned out that he "hyperventilated" while waiting for his first solo take-off.

While Nedra had experience with Air Force life by now, with the advent of Frank in pilot training, her anxiety was ratcheted up a bit. The Air Force was training a lot of pilots at Bartow AB, and Nedra was already experiencing the negative effects of being pregnant again, and flight training didn't help.

Nedra was pregnant at the time, and she was having "morning sickness". To help her feel better, she went to the Bartow AB Clinic, and was getting a glucose IV when the whole clinic staff ran out to go to the Gilbert Field crash site. Nedra knew that I was training at that auxiliary field that day, and prayed I was not the student who crashed.

Nedra recalls:

Six months flight training in Florida coincided with the conception of our second child, with lots of the usual morning sickness. This time, I became dehydrated and was on the table at the clinic getting a glucose IV when all the doctors disappeared. It was then I heard the dreaded words—"there has been a plane crash." My heart stopped. The nurse, realizing my husband was a pilot, assured me it was not my husband. We attended the funeral two days later—the student and his wife were newlyweds…The base officials were glad to see this class graduate: Three plane crashes and two pilots dead.

Although the movie, "Top Gun" was essentially a rather poor dramatization of life in military aviation, one aspect of the movie, at least, rings true: Getting back in the saddle. That, and the very real fact that "if you fly [planes] long enough, something like this is going to happen."

Per normal procedures, all flying stopped for a short while, till the crash victim could get taken care of. Another normal procedure in such cases has all the other students to fly right away, to lessen the fears that the crash could cause among the class. Our second fatality in Cub training involved two dual planes that collided in-flight while doing air work training. One plane landed safely, while the second one crashed. The instructor in the crashed plane stayed on the plane strut helping the student who was slow in opening his safety belt. By that time the plane was too low, and he was found dead sitting near the plane strut. The student he helped survived, since his parachute opened in time. I don't recall if the student continued in flight training after that, but these accidents were two real tragedies, but they would only be the beginning of the rather dangerous life as a military aviator.

At the time, Nedra was keeping the homefront going, tending to Steve and awaiting the birth of Carol, the Szachta's first daughter. Nedra seemed to really enjoy her role in support of Frank's career, and enjoyed more than anything being a homemaker. This seems in sharp contrast to her experience after high school graduation. Back then, all she could think about was living the good life, enjoying her time and taking care of Nedra. Obviously, once she met and fell in love with Frank, something happened inside her being, in her heart and soul.

Additionally, this was the Szachta's first brush with Florida; apparently, the suncoast area was greeted by them with great favor, as time will tell.

Pilot training continued as it has for generations, and as it still proceeds today. That is, pilot candidates move onward and upward; as they exhibit acceptable proficiency in one aircraft, they move up to a more sophisticated platform, each step a more complex, higher performance aircraft. Frank's next step in Primary Flight Training would be the North American T-6 "Texan." Thousands upon thousands of Air Force, Navy and Marine pilots flew the T-6 in primary flight training. The airplane responds well to a patient, smooth pilot, but will protest if a student tries to man-handle it.

Our training in the AT-6 Texan started well also. My solo went smoothly, but my halfway stage check with an Air Force pilot went poorly. I rounded out for a three point landing too high, and hit hard. He had me do it over, and I ended up landing hard three times in a row. As I got out of the front seat, and passed the Check Pilot while getting off the plane wing he said " I must be Santa Claus, since I am going to pass you: Boy was I relieved.

The final check flight went well and I graduated near the top of the class. I loved solo acrobatics, and my instructor, Mr. Johnson, a small fellow as well, sent me off many times and said, "have some fun" and I did. He helped me learn aerobatics early and frequently sent me off to practice loops, rolls, and Cuban eights. Since my instructor was small like me, we looked funny walking toward this big plane, with our parachutes, and two big cushions each!

I selected single-engine jet training as my advance pilot training assignment and we were sent to Greenville Air Force Base, Mississippi for our T-33 training. This location was hot and muggy, right along the Mississippi River. We were lucky to find a small 2-bedroom home to rent and luckier yet to find a maid to help Nedra with the housework, as she grew bigger with our second child. Pearly Mae was our maid's name, and she was great worker. Help in Greenville was very inexpensive, and Pearly worked all day for only $3. Nedra would ask Pearly to eat lunch with her every day she worked for her, but Pearly Mae refused, and preferred to eat alone outside, sitting on the garbage can. A sad commentary on southern living between black and

----

white people in the 50's.

Nedra writes:

Our next assignment was Greeneville, Mississippi for jet training for six months. Frank was zooming around the sky as I got bigger and bigger until the morning of August 9, 1956, when I woke him and said, "It's TIME!" Six hours later, Carol Marie made her appearance into our lives. *She is a biochemist and was part of a team at Pfizer. She now works at the Research Division at Washington Medical School, is mother of three and grandmother of three.*

It's interesting to note that, in her blog regarding Air Force life as it applies to families, Sarina Houston, wife of Air Force Captain Jacob Houston, counsels against either getting married or having children during pilot training![11]

My T-33 training went pretty well until we started formation training. We went on a cross-country flight during this period and my instructor "Batman" lost the formation during a penetration descent to Langley AFB, VA. He told me later that his formation flying abilities were mediocre and that to help me graduate, he was turning me over to another instructor. This Captain instructor was one of the Dr. Jeckle and Mr. Hyde type instructors I had heard about, but never met yet. These instructors are nice gentlemen on the ground, but once they get you into the

---

[11] http://www.vance.af.mil/news/story.asp?id=123356080

plane, they become cuss crazy idiots. I was shocked by his style, but he got me through formation training, and I thank him for that.

Since I made the top 10% of the class in grades, I got to select the type planes I would train in advance schools. We had a Strategic Air Command Bomber group of recruiters visit our base half way through our training, and they were recruiting pilots for the rear seat of the new B-47 Long Range Bomber, which was to become that "big stick" in the Cold War with Russia. Since I was married with children already, this nuclear deterrent force argument made sense to me. After their briefings, my mind turned toward that type training which meant "Navigator Training for Pilots" would be in our future. Thus as graduation loomed closer, I selected SAC and the B-47training for my advance pilot course.

Although hostilities ended in Korea in July of 1953, the world political climate was changing, the temperature rising. A crackerjack jet fighter pilot like Frank would be immediately called into any conflict that arose anywhere around the globe. Taking into consideration his wife and family—as well as having the vision to see what appeared to be a greater calling on the horizon, Frank opted to leave the speedy fighter behind and aimed for the B-47 strategic bomber. Of course, there was at least one stop on the way.

Since I was married and had a son already, the excitement and adventure of selecting the "fighter jockey" route after pilot training did not have the appeal for me, as it did for my bachelor classmates. The SAC recruiting team visited our T-33 training base and their pitch appealed to me since this mission represented our nation's first line of defense in the "Cold War". The B-47 was a very sleek looking bomber and the training for the copilot of this small 3-man crew involved a course called "Navigator Training for Pilots" (NTP) which qualified these pilots as "Triple Headed Monsters." That is, pilot, navigator, and bombardier. It sounded very patriotic and worthwhile to me, and I volunteered for this assignment. Thus, after graduation with my silver pilot wings, we left Greenville MS. in the winter of '56 and moved to James Connelly AFB, Waco, TX. for the NTP school. This six month long school during which we learned navigation and bombing/radar duties in the Convair T-29 as we also checked out in the B-25 bomber (of WWII fame for their carrier launched raid on Tokyo, lead by Lt. Col. Jimmy Doolittle) for multi-engine pilot proficiency. All new arrivals had to check out in the B-25.

Nedra writes:

Now the Air Force decides we need more training so six months "Navigator Training for Pilots", and Waco, Texas is our next home. I remember those nights of standing on the front lawn looking through a navigator's sextant, learning about the stars. Oh, by the way, I was into morning sickness again! But I could still identify Orion's Belt! We finished in Waco with me very pregnant with number 3 on our way to our next home in Tampa, Florida, and MacDill Air Force Base.

Any kind of separation is difficult for any loving family; for military families, even though separations are common and expected, they are no less difficult. Early on in their Air Force career, Frank and Nedra made a decision to remain together as a family wherever they went, unless the assignment did not allow it. Frank tells about it when he was sent to nuclear bombing school in Kansas:

Before we were made into a B-47 bomber crew at MacDill AFB, we were sent TDY (Temporary Duty Unassigned, a USAF acronym) in the fall of '58 to Wichita, Kansas for Nuclear Bombing Training. We didn't have much experience yet in family separations, but we felt enough risk for us, and were in love enough, that we were determined to keep them at a minimum. So, when we got these TDY orders, we decided to pack up our family of three youngsters, with infant Bob along, and drive north for this three month school. It wasn't too long into the school that we experienced the wisdom of our decision. A pilot training friend at the school also came alone, and soon a young lady we did not know snagged him and started to create problems. It was later cleared up a bit when his wife came north, but the problem haunted him for years afterward. We happily decided early on that unless orders forbid our staying together, we would do so, at all costs.

The school went quite fast. It was cold in the wintertime in flat Kansas, and we were sure the kids stayed wrapped up all the time we were outdoors. Since most of the nuclear bomb delivery course was classified, there was no homework or chit chat at home about school problems or issues. It turned out that much of my future career in the Air Force would be involved with nuclear bombs or the study of such subjects, that work stayed at work, and didn't involve home talk. The courses were typical military style, with multiple choice tests and these were quite easy for me after seeing so many of these type exams over the years. Before you know it, the school term was over, and we packed up the 56 Plymouth and headed back to Tampa, FL. and the Mac Dill AFB B-47 crew assignment.

We kept up our friendship with several pilot training friends and their families during this training. In particular the Dick and Mary Prescott family and the Sam and Mary Rose family. These friends made the same decision we did to become SAC crewmembers. The early days of this school were exciting for us "jet jockeys" as we had to train into the B-25 multi-engine prop plane in a few flights. The normal AF twin-engine pilots trained in the B-25 for six months, as we did in the T-33 Lockheed "Shooting Star" single engine jet plane. My friend Sam Rose and I trained together in the B-25, and after only about 5 flights our instructor shocked us by saying "OK, you guys are cleared to fly together, so it's all yours". We were shocked that after so short a training we would be given the plane as ours to fly alone. The Instructor continued, "You are wearing pilot wings, so go fly". We now know how some of the young WWII pilots must have felt. Since our flying involved carrying only us two pilots and no passengers, the instructor knew the risk of hurting anyone but ourselves was low. We were "target planes" for another B-25 loaded with radar and Air Defense Command (ADC) navigators training to be rocket-firing officers aboard ADC fighter aircraft. We would fly simple maneuvers called out by the "Fighter" B-25 trying to attack our "Target" plane. For instance the fighter/attack plane would call out an "A" and we would climb 1000ft while doing a left turning circle. Sam Rose and I had fun doing these flights together as we kept learning more about this complicated machine the instructor entrusted to us.

A few interesting events during these B-25 flights come to mind. Since the "fighter" B-25 plane had multi-engine instructor pilots aboard, who knew the low level of multiengine experience we "Target" pilots had in the B-25, they enjoyed playing tricks on us. On one dark night flight there was a strong jet stream blowing south at our flight altitude of 5000ft. The instructor pilots had us fly many climbing and descending turns, with little straight and level flying. Our main navigation radio in the stripped down plane we flew was a low frequency radio called a "bird dog", which has a receiving range of only about 20 miles. Since we did many turning maneuvers for over two hours, we were blown south over 100 miles from our base. When the instructors in the attack plane told us that they were done, they added "See you at the home base, we assumed we would just descend and land. We checked our "Bird Dog" radio for a heading to home base and saw a green and split white beacon on the airport very near our position. Since this is a military field type beacon, we assumed it was our base. The "Bird Dog" is a weak radio, and the needle seemed to be pointing in about the right direction. Since we alternated seats, Sam was in the pilot's seat this mission and entered a downwind leg for the base in sight. It didn't look right to me, and I told Sam "our compasses must be off 180 degrees since you are on downwind heading north, and the tower call at altitude said we are landing to the north". I also told Sam that the planes on the ramp all look small, like T-33's and not the B- 25 or T-29's we have on our home base ramp. At that time we both realized the trick our Attack plane instructors played on us is advising us to descend to home base, when they knew we were 100 miles south. This was Bryan AFB; my old base from enlisted days, and not James Connelly AFB, at Waco, TX. It just happens that Bryan and sister town College Station look like the city of Waco at night, and the weak radio beacons were nearly useless at the 100-mile distance we were at that night.

The Tower wasn't answering our radio calls for landing permission, since there was no night flying at Bryan, this night. Within minutes, we realized the trick the instructors played on us. The strong jet stream blew us over 100 miles south, and we were in the Bryan area when the instructors advised us that the tower told us to land north, as they advised us to descend. Once we realized we had been "tricked," Sam "firewalled" the throttles and we flew north as fast as we could. The instructor's plane beat us home easily, and we were really razzed at the next day's mission briefing. On our flight north after realizing our goof, Sam and I laughed so hard, it was tough keeping the plane on a smooth heading home.

Another interesting night flight involved the B-25 engines and their unique Holley variable Venturi carburetors. Since we were rather inexperienced in this plane and these engines and since most ADC training missions took place at night, we were prone to hear strange engine noises. This special engine/carburetor arrangement was prone to icing at the Venturi, in the carburetor in the humid spring air we were experiencing. The Holley variable Venturi also was prone to create engine detonation, with small adjustments of the engine. Detonation is an explosive knock in the engine cylinders that causes loss of power, just as the icing problem does also.

Couple this set of engine problems at the opposite end of the thermometer with our low experience levels and the night anxiety factor and you have a set of conditions sure to raise the "pucker factor" of these two pilots. One night we were in the traffic pattern at Waco, our home base when the engine started to lose power and sounded rough. Sam Rose yelled "carburetor ice" and I added carburetor heat. In a moment the engine got rough again and Sam said, "Check the cylinder temperature gauge for detonation", and it looked high, so I changed the Venturi setting. It seemed this went on for two or three cycles as we landed and called it a night. What a rough way to learn and get used to the operation of this unusual engine.

Our experiences in the T-29 aircraft were much different. This pressurized twin-engine plane was very modem compared to the B-25. We were training as navigator/bombardiers in this plane, thus all our missions in this plane involved us working at crew training stations in the rear cabin. This meant we did not work in the pilot compartment, but in the passenger section of a large plane. We would spend endless hours peering through drift meters as a navigation tool as well as periscopes' sextants to read the elevation of stars and other celestial bodies to determine where we were. We even had to take hand held sextants home to study the sky constellations so our sextant work would be easier to do the next night. It's still fun to look skyward at night and recognize "Orion's Belt" in the constellation Orion and realize the knowledge this presents. We later learned to study a radars circular scan and recognize the terrain and city features necessary to do bombardiers duties.

This work was necessary since the B-47 co-pilot was to use the sextant at his crew position by sliding it into his cabin canopy and "shoot the stars" for the navigator. We also learned how to use a large plastic Vaid Plotter to crudely plot our three star shots, to cross check the navigators plotting of the data we fed him minutes earlier. It turned out that the co-pilot was the "glue" that melded the three man crew into an entity in: assisting the navigator; reading all checklists to the whole crew; do the fuel management; turn his seat around to operate the tail guns by radar, like a "video game", before those words were invented; and operate the Electronic Countermeasures; and work all the radios. Sadly doing all these "Jack of all Trades tasks" left one little time to fly the plane. Doing all these sundry duties, the control column in his rear seat was stowed and gathering dust. In fact, the squadron had to schedule a purely training flight every few months so us co-pilots could do a few take-offs and landings from the rear seat. Thus many "backseaters" had to relearn our flying skills after leaving SAC.

After graduation from Navigator Training for Pilots (NTP) we were assigned to the 306th Bomb Wing at MacDill AFB, Tampa, FL. What a choice assignment, more luck again. This Bomb Wing was the first to get the B-47, and it was a mature and top notch Wing when we joined it in 1957.

CHAPTER EIGHT:
NUCLEAR FAMILY

MacDill AFB was established in 1939 as Southeast Air Base, Tampa. It is named in honor of Colonel Leslie MacDill (1889–1938). A World War I aviator, Colonel MacDill was killed in a crash of his North American BC-1 on 8 November 1938 at Anacostia, D.C. During World War I, he commanded an aerial gunnery school in St Jean de Monte, France. There are several dates surrounding the history of MacDill AFB. Official records report an establishment date of 24 May 1939, date construction began 6 September 1939, date of beneficial occupancy 11 March 1940 and formal dedication 16 April 1941. This last date is normally associated with the age of the base. It was renamed MacDill Field on 1 December 1939.

MacDill Field was one of two major Army Air Corps bases established in the Tampa Bay area in the buildup prior to World War II. Tampa's Drew Field Municipal Airport, established in 1928 was leased by the Air Corps in 1940. A major expansion of the airport was initiated and Drew Army Airfield was opened in 1941. Headquarters, Southeast Air District was first activated at MacDill Field on 18 December 1940. It was later re-designated HQ Third Air Force and moved to offices in downtown Tampa on 8 January 1941.

Two secondary Army Airfields, Brooksville Army Airfield and Hillsborough Army Airfield were built and opened in early 1942 to support the flight operations of MacDill and Drew Fields. The Bonita Springs Auxiliary Field, located near Fort Myers provided an additional emergency landing field for MacDill. All of these airfields came under the jurisdiction of Third Air Force. III Bomber Command, the bombardment arm of 3d Air Force was headquartered at MacDill Field. III Fighter Command, the fighter arm, was headquartered at Drew Field.[12]

The first lines of the United States' nuclear defense, B-47 Stratojet units were tasked with penetrating Soviet air defenses in the case of war and delivering nuclear weapons against a variety of targets. As a result, squadrons generally operated from forward bases in Great Britain, Greenland, Guam, Alaska, and Morocco. Due to the aircraft's strategic mission, it did not see action in the Korean War which was ongoing at the time of its introduction. The first two years of

---

[12] MacDill AFB, Official Site: www.macdill.af.mil

the B-47's career saw it continue to suffer from problems relating to takeoff/landing and low-altitude performance. Addressing these with the definitive B-47E, Boeing also added more powerful engines, improved avionics, ejection seats, and a stronger defensive armament. In addition, the aircraft's built-in jet-assisted takeoff (JATO) system was eliminated in favor of an expendable, external JATO rack.

Fully operational by 1953, the B-47 became a favorite of pilots who appreciated its fighter-like controls and performance. Due to their nuclear deterrence role, B-47 squadrons typically operated on one-third alert. This meant that one third of the aircraft were always armed, fueled, and ready for an immediate strike against the Soviet Union.[13]

Frank Recalls:

Since MacDill was very active at the time with two bomber wings and two refueler KC-97 Squadrons, there was no base housing available for young incoming crewmembers. We looked for rentals, and there was none of decent quality to be had. The next step was to look at homes under construction. As First Lieutenants, our budget for a new home was limited.

There were many small three-bedroom homes under construction in subdivision called Gandy Gardens, just north of the base near Dale Mabry Boulevard. One home we saw was nearly finished and it only cost $11,500, with a

---

[13] http://militaryhistory.about.com/od/ColdWarAircraft/p/Cold-War-Boeing-B-47-Stratojet.htm

down payment of $750 on a GI/VA loan. We needed a home quickly since Nedra was due our third child (to be Bob) any day now. Like our usual luck, this home at 4425 Montgomery had a grade school across the street and the base was only about two miles south. The front yard had a sinkhole full of water that worried us a bit, but it was a small defect we could handle since we needed a home right now. Son Bob came along a month after we moved in and the front yard was leveled by then, and Nedra's mother came down to help out, just in time. Bob was born on September 28, 1957.

Now, it was really getting exciting for Nedra. As the wife of an officer pilot, especially one who was about to embark on highly classified missions, her duties were about to expand, according to official U.S. Air Force guidelines.

Nedra writes:

Frank is now a co-pilot on a B-47 bomber, up there defending our country! I have been instructed that, as a "good" Air Force wife, I 'must get up and prepare breakfast at 4 A.M. so your husband has energy for his important flight. You must also never have an argument as this does not make for good flying.' I have coached my love in all the emergency procedures (memory work) on a B-47—I couldn't even identify the handles, but I know all the words! This I did between folding diapers and cooking dinner. My mother came for the birth this time; my other babies were 10-14 days early. This one, Robert (Bob), arrived a day late, after the traditional six hours of labor, on September 28, 1957. Bob is now a UPS driver with an impeccable safety record!

Now into a new aircraft, Frank had more training to do. He was delighted to have been teamed up with a veteran pilot and certified Instructor Pilot (IP) named Bill Ferreira. This matchup would allow Frank to get the necessary instruction to move into the A/C role.

After we returned to MacDill we were assigned a

crew position with Bill Ferreira as AC, me as CP and Jim Brown as Nav. We met Bill's wife Nel and his family as well as Pat Brown and their family. Bill had been an IP (Instructor Pilot) in the B-47 at Wichita and this was great since I would be able to swap seats with Bill during aerial refueling and upgrade to AC in the future. Bill still needed a local area checkout before we could begin crew missions and he was scheduled on a training flight on April 15, 1958 with another pilot an IP and a crew chief in the aisle seat. Due to gathering thunderstorms typical of Florida they removed the crew chief and flew the IP's Nav. up front to watch the radar and hopefully avoid the worst storms. They took off in the late afternoon, a typical time for storms in the region. As they took off on runway 22, their flight path heads them toward the Sunshine Skyway Bridge and their first turn point at Egmont Key, an island just west of the bridge. They hit a heavy thunderstorm shortly after take-off and a wing peeled off as they passed the bridge causeway. All four men were killed in this tragedy. It turned out many B-47's were crashing in a like way, since the wing flex at the wing tips is 13ft; and the Boeing engineers had little experience judging the life span of such a flexible wing structure. I was assigned as Summary Court Officer, which meant I was to help Nel, Bill's widow with his burial and all its details and help her in any way, needed. We became close friends with Nel and her family following this tragic event.[14]

    After this tragedy we were assigned a new AC

---

[14] The wings on all B-47's were thereafter retrofitted with unique stabilizer/reinforcements.

named George Howard Byram, and he preferred to be called Howard. He was a WWII veteran of the Pacific P-38 battles. We met his wife Helen and their daughters. Our crew training went well but I found out that Howard being older than Bill didn't want to become an IP, so that meant my future plans to upgrade to the front seat were not to be.

Upon his assignment to MacDill, Frank was also teamed up with Lieutenant James K. Brown, who rode the B-47 as Navigator/Bombardier. Jim was born in 1932 in Grove City, Pennsylvania, and, upon graduation from high school in 1950, worked for Lockheed Aircraft in California. After two years with Lockheed, Jim joined the Air Force in March of 1953, and earned his commission and Air Force wings in October of 1954. After a twenty-year career in the Air Force, Jim—who'd earned a BA and MA while in the Air force—went on to teach at the high school level, and also served as a high school guidance counselor.

Jim's illustrious career in the Air Force led him to a job in intelligence in Viet Nam, where he was Director of Targeting for Tactical Airstrikes in South Viet Nam and Laos. Jim and his wife, Patricia, whom he married on May 21, 1955, met Frank and Nedra when Jim was assigned to the 306th Bomber Wing at MacDill, and the four became lifelong friends. Jim writes:

By whatever the process, the three of us [with Major Howard G. Byram as Aircraft Commander] were assigned to become a combat-ready crew to the Strategic Air Command. With that assignment, we became a close-knit team with a very responsible mission ahead of us. On that day we became a team of 'ONE,' and functioned as 'ONE' for the next 4 1/2 years. 'Peace' was our profession, and our mission was to defend our nation from any foreign aggressor, as a deterrent force for the duration of the 'Cold War.'

Our daily routine included class training, Flight Simulator training, Mission and Flight planning and lengthy flight missions to hone our skills. [We performed] week-long tours of 'Alert' duty, both at MacDill AFB and overseas in Spain and North Africa. We were on duty round-the-clock, prepared to launch at a moment's notice, loaded with nuclear bombs.

Frank was very pleased to be teamed up with Jim and Howard, although, as pointed out earlier, Howard's lack of designation as an instructor pilot prevented Frank from gaining any flight time that could translate into a promotion as A/C in the future. Nevertheless, as Jim points out, the three functioned as a team, and Frank loved flying with them in the sleek "Statojet."

Frank writes:

Most of my first flights in the B-47 were made in the

4th man seat. It really wasn't a seat. The three crewmembers each had an ejection seat for emergencies, while the fourth man (usually a trainee or crew chief) sat on an aisle step in the zone between the two pilot seats.[15] There was a vertical entry door forward of the 4th man seat, and the navigator/bombardier sat forward in the nose compartment. The 4th man seat had no windows; all the training procedures come

---

[15] Earlier B-47 models had no ejection seat for a fourth crewmember. The fourth ejection seat was added in some models at a later date.

via the interphone radio. The three-crew members are all lined up in tandem with the navigator in the nose, The Aircraft Commander (A/C) above, and, behind him in the front cockpit, and the co-pilot behind the A/C in the aft canopy cockpit position. My first impression of these professional crews General LeMay had trained for SAC came while observing routine timing for take-off procedures witnessed from my aisle seat and hearing the interphone voices. I recall the mild bumps and turning sensations as we taxi out for takeoff on runway 04 at MacDill. This huge (500ft wide and 12,000ft long) runway is necessary since the B-47 has a high speed wing design that needs a 11,000 ft takeoff roll and an airspeed of 168 knots when fully loaded for a long overseas mission.

As we neared the take-off position, the Navigator (Nav) called out, "5 minutes". As we turned onto the runway and I could see the AC change the nose steering ratio for take-off, the Nav called out, "one minute". I now see the AC start to slowly move the six jet engine throttles forward as the brakes remain set. The Nav now calls out "ten seconds, then five, four, three, two, one and zero".

With the "Zero" call the A/C reaches 100% rpm on throttles and releases his brakes. He then reaches down and hits the water/alcohol augmentation switch for added thrust for 75 seconds of the take-off roll. The water creates the black smoke on take-off roll and gives the plane added thrust needed to speed the lift-off.[16] The Co-Pilot (CP) calls out "60 knots" so he and the AC can check their airspeed instruments. He next calls "103 knots, GO" which tells the AC that the planes acceleration is OK and that they are GO for the take-off. This decision comes early in the roll since the huge bomber has so much inertia that it cannot stop in the remaining runway. Any emergency that occurs from now on is treated as a flying/airborne emergency. This, my first observed B-47 take-off as seen from inside this slick bomber, was a real training experience which showed me the professionalism that I soon learned was present in all SAC crews and missions. Impressive, believe me.

As Co-Pilot, Frank had a number of duties, one of which was to arm the nuclear weapon, should the need arise. The Mark 6 "60-inch nuclear bomb" was the first atomic bomb to be mass produced by the United States. It was designed to be delivered by the heavy bombers of the Strategic Air Command and employed against strategic military targets only. The first version of the bomb was developed beginning in 1949 and first deployed in 1951. Several models of the Mark 6 were produced before it was finally removed from the nuclear stockpile in 1957. The

---

[16] The aircraft had what was known as a "horse collar" JATO rack (a jet-assisted takeoff setup) mounted just behind the aft (rear) wheel well and capable of having 33 JATO jet bottles on it. Each of those JATO bottles was in fact a 1000-pound-thrust rocket. Sampson Veteran's Tale - B-47 Stratojets and me - not quite love at first flight by William A. Ray; http://sampsonveteran.hubpages.com/hub/B-47-Stratojets-and-me-not-quite-love-at-first-flight

Mark 6 did serve, however, as the basis for the development of the Mark 18 nuclear weapon in the mid-1950s.

This weapon was a capsule bomb, meaning that the nuclear material for the bomb was kept in a special capsule separate from the rest of the device for safety's sake. Just before the bomb was to be dropped from the delivery aircraft the capsule was inserted into the bomb casing and the weapon became armed. It was also the first atomic weapon to offer the delivery aircraft's bombardier the option of changing the detonation altitude while the bomber was in flight to the target.[17]

Here Frank gives a detailed description of the arming operation:

The first thing the co-pilot had to do was to depressurize the cabin. Before doing so, he needed to ascertain that the oxygen bottle attached to his parachute system was full. He would disconnect his oxygen feed from the aircraft's oxygen feed and re-attach it to the oxygen bottle on his parachute harness. The other crewmembers would remain on the aircraft's oxygen system that was replenished by a large liquid oxygen cylinder (LOX) on the aircraft. Once the cabin was depressurized and the aircraft was approaching the "go/no go" point of the mission enroute to the target (somewhere inside the Soviet Union) the co-pilot would exit his seat and make way to the bomb

[17] http://www.globalsecurity.org/wmd/systems/mk6.htm

bay in the aft, center section of the plane, via a small door that could only be open safely after the depressurization of the aircraft.

The first order of business after we passed the "go/ no go" point (if we received a "go" order, which was verified for authenticity by at least two crewmembers), is the co-pilot would proceed into the bomb bay and move to the nose cone section of the bomb, and unscrew the nose cone from the Mark VI weapon. After he did that, he would reach into the trigger zone of the weapon and pull out a chain which was in the weapon, which would prevent the neutrons from commencing the expansion process. This expansion process, known as "fission," would take place as the weapon moved through the designated altitude. It would normally be triggered by an atmospheric pressure switch as it passed through approximately 10,000 feet. Once the co-pilot pulled this chain from the weapon's trigger section, he would place it in a secure location within the bomb bay. He would then remove the trigger from the same secure location. The trigger was a softball-sized metal capsule of plutonium, and this was screwed into the center section of the nose cone. After the plutonium was secured in the weapon, the co-pilot would replace the nose cone of the weapon. Once this operation was complete, "armed" lights would come on on the A/C's panel, indicating to him that the weapon was armed and ready for deployment. Then the co-pilot would reverse his actions until his oxygen mask was reconnected to the aircraft's oxygen system and the A/C could then commence the process of re-pressurizing the crew compartment.

As you can see, the Mark 6 was an antiquated weapon of the World War II variety that we were still using at that time.

While her husband was busy handling dangerous, potentially-catastrophic plutonium, Nedra was on the homefront—occasionally diffusing "bombs" of a different— albeit somewhat less volatile--variety. Being the ever present "good Air Force wife," Nedra still had duties of her own. With three children already, and a fourth on the way, she most definitely had her hands full. Thirteen months after the birth of little Bob, Nedra gave birth to another child she named Jeanne. Frank was already in the duty rotation for his squadron, which meant 23-day deployments to Zaragoza, Spain. Initially, these deployments were 90-day durations, however, General Lemay, under advisement, decided that the three month period was too long for pilots to be separated from their families, and shortened the assignments to three weeks. These overseas deployments involved flying long-duration missions on planned routes that remain classified to this day. However, suffice to say that the B-47's mission was to be ready to retaliate against the Soviet Union. The bombers were the first line of America's strategic nuclear deterrent, often operating from forward bases in the UK, Morocco, Spain, Alaska, Greenland and Guam. B-47s were often set up on "one- third" alert, with a third of the operational aircraft available sitting on hardstands or an alert ramp adjacent to the runway, loaded with fuel and nuclear weapons, crews on standby, ready to attack the USSR at short notice.

In his excellent book, <u>Ideologies in Conflict: A Cold-War Docu-Story,</u>[18] Air Force Major General Chris Adams provides some background with regard to these "Reflex" missions, as quoted by Major General Earl Peck:

"The typical B-47 mission was comprised of all those activities that the crew had to master if the system was to serve as a credible deterrent; they were also the same things that would be required during a nuclear strike mission if deterrence failed: high and low level navigation and weapon delivery, aerial refueling, electronic countermeasures against air and ground threats, positive control procedures, exercising the tail mounted 20 millimeter guns, emergency procedures, cell (formation) tactics, and others I am sure I've forgotten. Crew planning for a mission took up most of the day prior and was elaborately precise and detailed. The crew was expected to approach each training with the same meticulous professionalism that would be required for an aerial strike mission. Professionalism came out of the mission attitude that prevailed from inception to completion. On the day of the flight there were an exhaustive series of inspections, exterior and interior perusal of forms, equipment and safety items, walk around inspection of aircraft system by system, interior inspection..."

---

[18] Adams, Chris, <u>Ideologies in Conflict: A Cold War Docu-Story</u>, IUniverse, 2001

Prior to the crew's first deployment in Spain, Nedra opined to Jim Brown about being a mother in Spain. Since the only religion in Spain is Roman Catholicism, Nedra surmised that every young woman there would either be pregnant or have a child in her arms (a thought possibly spurred by her own early-marriage condition). Upon their arrival, Frank had the opportunity to go to town to either confirm or dash Nedra's suspicions. Of course, Frank discovered that Nedra's suppositions were not true!

Conversely, Nedra seemed to be often with child, and, unfortunately, Frank was on just such a deployment when Jeanne was born on October 23, 1958, three weeks early.

I warned our Squadron Commander Lt. Col. Childress that Nedra usually delivers early and that our crews' next scheduled "Reflex" overseas trip to Zaragoza, Spain would have us away at the baby's birth. "Don't worry" he said, we can get you home early if needed. I wasn't happy, but off we flew to Zaragoza for our scheduled reflex trip. These trips are 23 days long with 7 days alert duty, 6 days of for rest and relaxation (R&R), and another 7 days alert duty before our return trip. During our six-day R&R the base often has a C-47 plane to fly the crews to a European vacation site. This trip, there was no C-47, so we planned a train trip to Barcelona, Spain and then a boat ride to the island vacation site of Palma in the Mediterranean ocean. Well, as we started our R&R, we arrived in Barcelona and were in a hotel awaiting the next day's boat ride to Palma. At 11pm the phone rings in our hotel room, and I know that Nedra has had our baby. I was right, and how they found us, is another "lucky break", I'm sure. I immediately made train reservations to return to our base in the hopes I could switch with another CP and get back to Nedra's side a week early.

Howard and Jim were going to continue their R&R to Palma. Well, the CP who could switch with me had to switch the previous month also, and as long as Nedra and child were healthy, I was out of luck, no switch. I recall the morning before while awaiting the train, as I wrote Nedra a short letter, sitting in a Barcelona park, expressing my sorrow for not being there with her. So, I had to wait a week for Jim and Howard's return from R&R, so we could pull our second week of Alert duty and then finally fly home to Nedra's side. I was one morose puppy, I can tell you. Nedra had delivered daughter Jeanne, the first (and only) delivery I missed.

Jeanne was two weeks old when Frank arrived home, but Nedra's mother had been with her the whole time.

Nedra writes:

In case you haven't been counting, we now had four children—and the oldest was only five years old! And I was only 25!!! Jeanne's now a graphic artist, living in the greater

St. Louis area.

On yet another "Reflex" mission, Frank wasn't there when Nedra received some troubling information from their pediatrician.

Nedra recalls:

When Jeanne was about three months old, our pediatrician diagnosed a problem. She would need skull surgery, as her "soft spots" had closed prematurely, which could cause blindness and other problems with development. My mother came back to stay with our other three children while we took her to Texas for the surgery. The surgery was successful, but she developed a bad virus. Back in Tampa, she was in critical condition for 29 days. Prayers were really flowing at that time; *even the doctor who delivered Bob came every day to pray by her crib while she was in the hospital.* She finally responded to cortisone treatment and we brought her home—tiny and loveable. Whether or not she had any residual problems was resolved when, in Hazelton Central High School, Jeanne became the first girl president of the National Honor Society!

Frank was in Spain, once again, when the diagnosis was made.

Three months later we were in Spain again on another "Reflex" trip. This time, we were scheduled to stay over an extra weekend so that bombloading crews at the base could practice on our plane. As we were in the Officers club having a happy hour drink on Friday evening, Howard got an emergency phone call to return to MacDill immediately. We knew of no reason for this change in plans. We couldn't go at once, because of the "eight hours between bottle and throttle" rule.[19] Jim and I pressed Howard for the reason for this rushed change of plans, but he wouldn't tell us anything. We thought a family member had been killed in an auto accident or some other such crazy thought. Finally the next morning Howard broke down and explained the reason for our rush trip back home. He told us

---

[19] FAA Regulation 91.17

that Jeanne, our daughter born during our past Reflex trip, had undergone a "well baby" check at the base hospital and was found to have prematurely early closing of her baby "soft spots" on her skull. Nedra was distraught, of course, and the Squadron felt we should get home as soon as possible. Jeanne would need surgery, likely at the big Air Force Hospital in San Antonio.

Our trip home went smoothly and we arrived home Saturday afternoon. It seemed that the doctor wanted Jeanne to have skull surgery at the Wolford Hospital in Texas, as we expected, but they had made no plans for our trip there. Finally two weeks later, Nedra and I were aboard a flight to Texas with baby Jeanne. Her condition was called Craniosynostosis, and corrective surgery calls for a slot to be made in her skull with plastic plug inserts so the slot will be new "soft spot" and that her skull growth can continue and her brain will be properly shaped. If the operation were not done, she could have a pin head or boat head, and the brain deformity caused by these conditions could yield vision or other problems later in life. The surgery went well and her recovery was very fast. We were amazed at the more serious baby problems being cared for at this fine hospital. We thanked the Lord for her good care and swift recovery, and for the other more seriously ill children being handled there.

In post-op care, baby Jeanne recovered fast, but the hospital in Texas was enduring a virus that caused a rash of diarrhea cases, and the staff felt we should get her out of that area as soon as we could. Her condition deteriorated during our plans to leave, and we traveled home with one sick girl. Her condition went up and down daily when we got back to the MacDill hospital, and we were worried that we may have to bury her in Tampa. Her birthing doctor prayed by her bedside daily, and slow but sure, she pulled out of this deathly illness. We know the Lord helped us pull through this emergency. The scar tissue over her soft spot feels like the Rocky Mountains, but she grew up to be healthy and went on to become a brilliant artist.

God's blessings have been countless, but we sure know how to count this one among them.

As the 1950's came to a close, the Air Force became very keen on a new bomber, the B-52 Stratofortress. Taking what it had learned in the development of the B-47, Boeing applied that knowledge into the development of what would become the flagship of the Strategic Air Command's long-range, high-altitude bombing mission. The B-52 has played a strategic role in every U.S. engagement since 1956, and the Air Force intends to continue to utilize these aircraft through 2045, 90 years after their first flights.

At this point, Frank Szachta had a decision to make. At Frank's suggestion, Jim Brown, Frank's Navigator, opted for further education and moved into the B-52, eventually overseeing missions during the Viet Nam conflict. Frank had always had an understanding that knowledge is power, and after discussing the matter with Nedra, he made a plan.

I decided that my earlier plans to start night school toward a possible future assignment to the Air Force Institute of Technology (AFIT) for a college degree were a good idea. I knew that such an education would enhance my promotion chances while also providing good insurance for a post-Air Force career. I checked on the AFIT requirements and found that I needed a year of college credits to qualify for AFIT acceptance. After checking with the Base Education office I found my best option lay with an engineering degree. There were several end-of-course exams the education office recommended that, when combined with a full Mathematics Night School schedule offered my best shot for AFIT acceptance. The University of South Florida, Tampa campus offered many math courses and their on-base campus had many professors that understood our difficult flight crew schedules. These staff helped me tremendously by sending work overseas with us as well as allowing absences due to flight crew duties that would normally cause a course grade of "F" for a regular night school student.

After a year of such classes I convinced Jim Brown our Navigator that he should start such courses. He soon was enrolled much heavier than I was. He selected another path to a college degree called the "Bootstrap" program. In this case, you enter full time college, with a year remaining, and the Air Force gives you a year leave at full pay to complete your degree program. Jim's accelerated program served him well since he was off to Bootstrap a few years later and got an education degree. His post-AF career was as a high school counselor, and he enjoyed it and was very happy with his efforts and career path.

The Browns and the Szachtas had become close friends. The family atmosphere of the Air Force translated naturally to off-duty time, as the couples and their families spent much time together.

Jim writes:

Since we all lived in close proximity to one another, togetherness was common. Howard had an indoor pool that offered great relaxation to all throughout the entire year. During the summers, we had great beaches for family enjoyment, and also had frequent picnics, cookouts and many activities for the children. Through it all, we became close, loyal friends and got to know everyone as "family."

Speaking of the families, one cannot diminish the importance of the wives who manage the households, tend to the needs of the children, and provide vital support to their husbands and their duties. Jim Brown says,

The men made up the operational "combat crew," with our focus on Mission, Performance and Dedication to our profession. To us, Peace was our "profession," while excellence and performance as a combat crew was our "Mission." Likewise, the wives fit beautifully into both military lifestyle and family lifestyle. To Nedra, Marriage and Homemaker was her "profession"; Family dedication and raising outstanding children in a supportive, loving and successful lifestyle was her "Mission"...Nedra was the co-pilot on their "crew."

One of the benefits of being on Alert status in Spain was the week of R&R the crew enjoyed at the conclusion of each deployment. Jim Brown writes:

Our travels included London, Madrid, Barcelona, Andorra; played golf on the Sultan's course in Morocco, saw snake charmers in Marrakesh, Flamenco dancers in Spain and the pleasant joys of Majorca. It was in Majorca where Frank got to sit in on the drums with a band, his "claim to fame," so to speak. It was the thrill of a lifetime for a young man from Buffalo! He wanted to go back the next night, buy Howard and I didn't wake him from a nap in time, and Frank was upset to say the least. He said, "Friends to the end; and THIS is THE END!" His bubble had been burst, and it was all our fault.

By 1962, the handwriting was on the wall for the B-47, and Frank had amassed sufficient credits from USF to apply to the Air Force Institute of Technology (AFIT). Performing admirably at USF, Frank was quickly accepted, and began to peruse the available civilian institutions that handled AFIT students. Due to the lack of cold weather apparel for the children, Frank applied to a number of schools in the southwest U.S., and some others. The Air Force, once again, had other plans. Frank was due to begin classes towards his BSEE (Bachelor of Science, Electrical Engineering) at the University of New Hampshire, located in Dover, near the Maine border.

Word had begun to circulate that MacDill AFB was going to close. Whether that was true or not, it was obvious to Frank that the base was in a "shrinking mode." In fact, Frank's squadron had already been slated to move to Texas.

Meantime, other bases were having trouble keeping their alert planes full of crews, and we were sent to Texas to help another Bomb Wing keep their alert planes on duty. So, with our AFIT tour assignment coming through soon, our crew, wives and all went on a huge party the night before we were to depart for Texas. We partied so heavily, that they had to drag us up the ladder of the KC-97 Tanker plane that was flying us to our alert TDY in Texas. A week later, we were sitting at the 0800-hours alert briefing in Texas when I spotted my replacement co-pilot peeking into the alert room window.

I motioned him in, shook hands with Jim and Howard, my crewmates for the last four plus years, and left for the flight home to family and our move to the college assignment. A sad and abrupt way to leave my SAC crew comrades and friends, but we have stayed friends to this day.

CHAPTER NINE : FRANK GOES TO COLLEGE

The Air Force Institute of Technology, or AFIT, is the Air Force's graduate school of engineering and management as well as its institution for technical professional continuing education. A component of Air University and Air Education and Training Command, AFIT is committed to providing defense-focused graduate and professional continuing education and research to sustain the technological supremacy of America's air and space forces.

AFIT accomplishes this mission through three resident schools: the Graduate School of Engineering and Management, the School of Systems and Logistics, and the Civil Engineer and Services School. Through its Civilian

Institution Programs, AFIT also manages the educational programs of officers enrolled in civilian universities, research centers, hospitals, and industrial organizations. Since resident degrees were first granted in 1956, more than 17,500 graduate and 600 doctors of philosophy degrees have been awarded.[20]

The single requirement for admission is that a student must have already completed one year of college. Frank had, in the time between 1957 and 1962, attended night school at the University of South Florida, and had hoped for an assignment for the balance of his education to be at a southwestern U.S. college, because the family had no wardrobe for colder weather. Frank could have gone to the Air Force's in-house AFIT at Wright-Patterson AFB in Dayton, Ohio, however he wanted a civilian college "so I wouldn't have to wear my uniform to class." Well, Frank got half of his wish.

At this time, Frank's "job" in the Air Force was as a college student—at the University of New Hampshire in Durham, New Hampshire. Let's let Frank tell us about how it all happened...

I had asked for an assignment to eight schools in the southwest, as the children had no winter clothing. Well, in the wisdom of the military, the University of New Hampshire had just started a small AFIT-associated program and our class was added to that program.

---

[20] http://www.afit.edu/ABOUT/index.cfm

I then flew back to Mac Dill AFB, Florida, via commercial air. Upon arrival, Nedra and I hugged a lot, and started packing for our move north to the University of New Hampshire. I was scheduled to report in May 62, to seek a Bachelor of Science degree in Electrical Engineering (BSEE) by 1964. A challenging goal, since the only college credits I held were from night school classes at South FL College of Tampa, in math, and a few end of correspondence courses I took through AFIT. This 27-month assignment meant college classes year round.

One interesting note, the school had made the assumption that those of us who had had night school and had been on active duty would comprise the lowest levels of the class, and we were assigned classes based upon that assumption. However, when the degree program was over, it turned out that those of us who had gone to night school while on active duty—and were still fulfilling pilot and navigator duties while enrolled in the university—reversed that list, and we all graduated near the top of the class!

We arrived up north in mid-May and were surprised to find some snow still on the ground in shady spots. We found a place to live through the listing on base at Pease AFB, NH. The home was across the border in South Berwick, Maine, and was owned by an Air Force officer who planned to make it his home after retirement. It was a lovely and large two-story colonial built in 1742. The house was nice and roomy, and served our family of six just fine. There was a large fireplace centrally placed that opened in two rooms at both levels, and had two blocked openings also. The rent was only $90 per month, and we took the lease (he only offered a year at a time) right away. The cellar had bare earth floors, and the home support rafters were rough hewn logs. There was even a small, skinny door into a small wine-cellar type room. As we opened the door we all expected to see a British redcoat fall forward, so typical of the Revolutionary War period that these conditions reminded us of.

As our moving truck arrived a few days later, a neighborhood fuel delivery truck came by and asked if we wanted to top off the fuel tank for our furnace? We agreed since a full tank leaves less room for moisture to form, and contaminate the fuel oil, as well as corrode the fuel tank. The fuel tank was buried under the front lawn, and as the truck was pumping the fuel oil into the tank, I asked the driver how many gallons he thought we would need. He answered "this truck ought to it" in his dry Mainers twang. I though, holy cow, this is a lot of fuel. In FL., our concrete block home had only a 55-gallon fuel tank to serve the small kerosene stove that sat in the central hallway, and heated the entire small 3-bedroom home. This home was about three times larger, and faced the cold Maine winters, so we soon learned the consumption of fuel oil was humungous. Fortunately, the prices were lower then, and the truck load cost only about $75, as I recall. With all rooms being huge, we did have an advantage of 7-foot ceilings, which helped save on heating bills. The home had a walk-through summer kitchen (which I had never heard of) and then you passed a 6-holer outhouse enroute to the huge barn. Three of the outhouse holes were lower for children, and three were higher level adult outhouse seats. Of course these were not in use, since indoor plumbing was added in the 30's, as well as the steam furnace and room radiators for the hot water, winter heating.

South Berwick was a small Maine town of about 1500 residents, I would guess, just across the river (state border) from Dover New Hampshire. Both these towns were about 10 miles west of Portsmouth, NH, the large city near Pease AFB, NH where I would keep up my pilot proficiency while attending college. The University of New Hampshire was at Durham, NH, a small town about 5 miles southwest of Dover, NH. All in all a nice compact arrangement, since snowy and cold winter driving made driving long distances a tough ordeal.

Nedra, still holding down the fort at home, had this to say:

In 1962, Frank was assigned to go to college at the University of New Hampshire—a lucky break since most men leave SAC in a casket! We spent the next 39 months with Frank studying all the time and flying on the weekends —this was during the Cuban Missile Crisis. I was up to my knees in snow, but I couldn't see them because—you guess it—I was pregnant with number 5. Frank, Jr. was born on December 26, 1963—followed by Evelyn, number 6, fifteen months later on March 20, 1965.

Six children, ages 10 thru newborn, sounds terribly daunting, particularly in today's world. Add in a husband who was up to his ears in books and away every weekend on duty flights, and one can imagine how easy it would be to say—"No More!" But Nedra wasn't cut out that way, and, as pointed out earlier, she wouldn't have traded places with anyone. Even after what she went through with Frank, Jr...

At 51 years old, Frank Jr. operates an alcohol and drug treatment facility for teens near Denver, Colorado. Sober for over 30 years now, "Frankie," as everyone in the family refers to him, became addicted to alcohol and other substances at a perilously early age. When I interviewed him for this book, he sat across from me at his father's table in Parrish, Florida and presented as a wise, humbled man. His long hair tied into a pony tail, a pack of cigarettes and a can of Coke in front of him, Frank Jr. told me about his battle with the bottle beginning at age 13, how it taxed the patience (and wallet) of his parents, how their attention to him ignited feelings of abandonment in his siblings, and how deep and unconditional love finally won. During that time, Frank Jr. says, Nedra described the phone by her bed as a "snake, coiled and ready to strike;" too often, in the middle of the night, it did. "I'd been arrested for something alcohol or drug related, Mom would answer, and Dad would dutifully drive to the precinct to bail me out of jail, again." On the drive home, not much was said. "I just wanted to get home and get to bed," Frank, Jr. says, "but Mom had other ideas. I'd walk in the door, and there was Mom, at the breakfast bar, in her nightgown and robe, with bed head: 'Sit down, we're gonna talk!'"

Nedra was the hub of the family, and when her child was in trouble, she wanted to find a way to fix it. "Things always happened when Dad was gone," according to Frankie (a sentiment echoed by other siblings). In fact, Nedra had "six or seven panic attacks," while Frank was deployed. Anxiety disorder, which causes what people call "panic attacks," is a very real brain response to stressful situations. In the midst of handling her home and family, and supporting Frank, Sr.'s career, it is not at all surprising that Nedra reacted with occasional panic attacks, the symptoms of which mimic that of a heart attack. Frequently, sufferers will demand to be taken to the emergency room thinking he or she is having a heart attack.[21] Nedra would summon her friend, Gail, to take her to the local hospital, to find out that she was having a panic attack and not a heart attack.

After a number of stints at rehab, Frank, Jr. convinced his parents that he was sober, though he was not. Particularly adept at carefully removing the tax labels from his parents gin bottles, Frank, Jr. would then deplete the contents by half or so, refill the bottles with water, and deftly replace the tax label around the cap with Elmer's glue ("My parents drank 20-proof gin for years!"). On one occasion, when Frank, Sr. and Nedra were away from the house on a long weekend, Frank, Jr. took advantage of the occasion by drinking his parents' gin in this fashion. He'd thought of it as an "experiment" to determine if he could

---

[21] http://www.webmd.com/anxiety-panic/guide/mental-health-anxiety-disorders

drink again, after being alcohol-sober for some nine months.

At some point, when the parents' return was imminent, Frank, Jr. thought it might be a good idea to mow the lawn to demonstrate to his parents that he was "being good," but the mower and the gas can were empty. No problem, decided Frank, Jr., who, with five or six shots of gin in him, set out to procure some gas in his 1971 Cutlass convertible. Not far from the house, Frank, Jr. realized he'd left without the gas can, turned around and prepared to make a quick grab of the gas can in the garage. Opening the driver's door and slipping out of the car should not have been a problem; however Frank, Jr. failed to place the vehicle in park first. With its jacked up idle settings, the old automobile continued into the garage and through the back concrete wall!

When asked by his mother whether he'd been drinking, Frank, Jr., figuring that this would absolutely be the last straw, swore he had not. Months later, when he finally admitted he'd been drinking at the time of the crash, his mother confirmed it; she would have tossed him out for good.

Ironically, the one habit Frank, Jr. still holds on to is nicotine. Ironic because it is the same habit his mother refused to give up, even after doctors had diagnosed her with COPD and heart disease. Two weeks before Nedra's death, her sister-on-law Mary Kimberlin spoke with her on the phone. "She told me she was fine, but I could tell she wasn't. She didn't laugh as much, and something was different about her. I don't know if she had a premonition

----

that she was going to die or whatever, but I could tell she wasn't the same Nedra. Still, though, I could hear her taking drags off a cigarette."

New Hampshire was a particularly difficult time— or should have been—for the Szachtas. Frank was in class all week long and flying all weekend. Most of the children have little recollection of their father during their three years there. Still, Nedra held it all together with a certain zest for life.

While in New Hampshire, Frank was still required to maintain his flying status and continue to build flying hours. Although the base was home to a B-47 squadron, Frank was not assigned to that squadron since he was no longer on "active" flight status, being a full-time college student. He would need to be checked out in another aircraft for flight time.

I checked into the base support-flying unit quickly. It was in the SAC and part of the 509th Bomb Wing (Bomber Wing), flying the B-47, as I did in FL in the 306th Bomber Wing. I learned that the Support Squadron helped the Bomber Wing and also supported the SAC 8th Air Force located at Westover AFB, not too far away. The support planes available to us AFIT college students for maintaining our flight proficiency were the T-33 "Shooting Star" a single engine jet trainer that many of us flew in pilot training. The other plane was the C-47 "Gooney Bird" also known in civilian circles as the DC-3, which made air travel popular in the late 30's and early 40's. It also was most famous for the WWII activities especially during the D-Day invasions of Europe. I selected the Gooney Bird, since the USAF and military were in a "between wars" period, and I was low on flying time. The missions the C-47 flew were often 6 to 8 hours long, while the T-33 missions were only 1-2 hours in duration. Thus, I could build hours toward my goal of 2000 hours by 7 years rated period, necessary for the senior pilot's star. We all knew that these milestones were important in the USAF if you wanted to stay in a flying status your whole career. In SAC, many of us were low on flying hours due to the many "Alert" periods we served, where your week in the Alert barracks yielded zero hours for your logbook.

Alert duty required us to remain in the Alert Quarters, or "mole hole" (since it was halfway underground so as to limit the noise of the airfield for those who were sleeping during Alert). We would brief each day at 0800 hours, and then wait. When the Claxon sounded, that meant we were to run to the aircraft, start the engines, turn on the radios, and report in "ready to taxi." And, on occasion, the highest level of our Alert duty would be nothing more than a taxi to the runway. That didn't happen very often; usually we just started the engines and reported "ready to taxi," so as to ensure good starting procedure in the case of an actual Alert. Therefore, as I said, we didn't get much logged flying time.

One of my classmates in college was a major Bob Childress who was an Instructor Pilot (IP) in the C-47 (the civilian equivalent is the McDonnell-Douglas DC-3), and he agreed to check me out in the Gooney Bird quickly, so I could start building up some needed flying time.

Major Bob Childress had over 5000 hours in the

C-47, and he rapidly started to check out all of the AFIT college students that preferred to fly the Gooney bird C-47 over the Shooting Star T-33. The C-47 was a DC-3 in early airline days, and could carry a big cargo load or about 25 passengers or a weight combination of these loads. On weekends in college we would frequently fly 6- or 7-hour cross-country flight to Miami, FL, New Orleans, LA, and once even to Los Angeles, CA. In this way we built up our flying hours fast.

Bob checked me out in only about 7 or 8 flights, and I still felt quite inexperienced in this complex and big plane. It was somewhat different from the speedy little T-33, which had power assist with the controls. The C-47 had no assist, and it therefore required good throttle control as well as a good deal of muscle, particularly at lower airspeeds and during the takeoff run. Well, as luck would have it, the 8th Air Force Inspector General (IG) team hit our base for a "No Notice" inspection. The pilot examiner wanted to fly with several base support pilots, and in particular with one of the most recently checked out pilots. Since I had not flown any flights since my check out in the C-47, I was selected for a check flight with the IG check pilot. I am sure I was a bit tense as the flight began. The flight seemed to go smoothly until he had me fly a non-directional beacon instrument approach at Manchester, NH airport near Pease AFB. The clouds were quite low, and I worked hard staying lined up on the wiggly low frequency beacon that made up the approach. Since I was inexperienced in low approaches in the low-level clouds we had that day, I made my approach, and just as we neared the "decision height" near the airport, the Check Pilot told me to "take it around." A few minutes later he told me to fly us back to Pease AFB. I couldn't figure out if something was wrong or what.

After we landed, I watched him fill out the Check Ride form, and noted he checked the "Failed" box. During the debriefing he told me that you must lower the landing gear before passing the Final Approach Fix, which I did not do. It was the first Check Ride I ever failed in my USAF flying days, and I was disappointed. In discussions with my instructor Bob in the next few days, he encouraged me by saying, "that I was unlucky to get a check ride so soon after checkout in the C-47, and that not to worry, in the he would give me a few more training rides, and be re-qualified at once." This sounded encouraging, and I was to learn soon, that Bob considered me instructor material, and within another 3 months, he made me his newest Instructor Pilot (IP). I really appreciated his confidence in my flying abilities, and I worked hard to get additional flying hours and check out many of the AFIT college students joining us at UNH and at Pease AFB in the following years.

One more thing I want to say about flying the C-47 "Goonie Bird" in New Hampshire. Because the weather was often not good, especially in winter, the Air Force had a top-notch group of Air Traffic Controllers stationed at Pease. On approach to landing in low-visibility and even stormy conditions—this is long before electronic approaches—the pilots and the controllers stayed in great contact, with the controllers providing the flight crew with instructions for flying and corrections on approach to keep the airplane on

----

the runway centerline and the proper glide slope for a safe landing.

Frank was flying high, in more ways than one. Living the dream, some might say. Getting a free college education and flying all over the country on the weekends was most likely not something contemplated by that seven year-old tyke from Buffalo. Which placed Nedra in the position of, essentially, a single parent. It is likely she never would have characterized herself as such, but the reality is found in what Frank once said to me, which is, "Nedra was 90 percent of the family."

I spoke about this with Bob, the Szachta's now 57-year old son. He told me he was always impressed with Nedra's unique ability to deal with each of her children as individuals. "Mom just knew how to handle each of us, because we were all different. She knew when to lift us up when we needed it, and when to challenge us. She drew lines for each of us—and we crossed them!"

Robert Szachta was born in Tampa in 1957, married his high school sweetheart after the family had moved to St. Louis, and signed on with UPS, the company he still calls his employer. Thirty-five years as a driver for the company without a single accident is a remarkable record. The marriage lasted 26 years, and produced two daughters. Now 25 and 29, the girls have their own lives and families. Bob's thinking about retirement, one that may include Florida, for he loves his golf.

Bob remembers his mom as having a "hands-off" approach to the various issues and problems faced by her children. Having the innate ability to remain neutral, providing a sounding board rather than a "fixer" or an advisor, Nedra—perhaps unbeknownst to the children at the time—provided the space and time each needed to thoughtfully consider the issue or problem and to arrive at his or her own conclusions and solutions. That's somewhat unique for an active, concerned and loving mom, who just wants her children to be happy. But it's obvious that Nedra, like her husband, possessed a respect for the power of intellectually handling the unpacking process of often emotionally-charged matters. They each knew that using the brain—the king of the body—always will produce the best course of action, no matter how heartfelt the problem might be. By their example, their children also gained respect for the process as well.

In so doing, Bob says, "They provided for us without any guilt trips; anything we needed, we had. I wanted bologna and mayonnaise for lunch, and that's what I got. Until I changed to bologna and mustard, and then I got that!"

"I'm a little like my mom, and a little like my dad. In some ways, I'm understanding and patient, like Mom. In other ways, I like to figure things out, you know, use my brain, like Dad. I think some of the kids are more like Mom, and some are more like Dad. But I'm really a half and half."

Each of the children—as Frank noted in his own immediate family growing up—sees the parents differently, has certain memories that, perhaps, even the other siblings *don't readily recall. And they each have a personal anecdote to share. Here's Bob's:*

"He thought about us kids at different times; you know, looked at us and tried to figure out what our strengths and weaknesses were. He saw that I was probably not going to be a college kid, that I was the kid who wanted to make money, buy a car, you know, just that kind of kid. He saw that in me, that I wanted to make money on my own, and he looked around for something I could sell.

"Well, there was this battery additive, and Dad had gone out and bought this box of battery additive, and came up with this name, "F & B," you know, Frank and Bob Enterprises, or whatever," he chuckles, "and this'll be great. 'Me and Bob will get closer' and I was kind of impressed. He was thinking about me. Well, I went out to sell it, and the first gas station I went to had a box of this stuff at like half-price, and I'm like 'Great.' You know, a sixteen-year-old kid and I don't know nothin' about sales. But, here's someone who's giving it away and I know I can't compete with that. So, another of Dad's ideas, shot down, as he realized 'well, this kid's not a salesman,' maybe, but he was thinking about me, made an effort. And he just moved on to another idea for me, whereas, I'm not sure I'd be the same way with my own kid."

Frank may have been absent a lot of the time, but he still made a way to be a guide and a motivator in his children's lives. Nedra, being home and highly present, seemed, perhaps, more reliable to the children.

Says Bob, "We knew we could go to Mom and she would be able to understand what the conflict was or how to motivate us out of a bad place, in a very natural way."

That said, Bob thinks the move to retire in Florida was a "good idea" for Nedra; she believed her influence in her adult children's lives was becoming too great, and it was "time to let them live their own lives." Nedra had established herself as the hub or referee of the family, out of a mother's instinctual desire to see her children safe and happy. In fact, the eventual move to Florida, according to Bob, "may have been to excise herself from that role, to remove herself as the crutch that the rest of us leaned on, so that we could move on with our lives as adults. And, to allow her to have a life of her own."

Florida and retirement was still a long way off when the family was in New Hampshire. There were still many years of Air Force life yet ahead, so let's let Frank tell more about that.

After we started college at UNH, our USAF-AFIT assignment, Nedra was beginning to get bored. I was busy going to school all day, studying most of every night, and flying and instructing in flying in the Gooney Bird (DC-3) at Pease AFB most week-ends. With me being so busy, Nedra was with our four children day in day out and needed some change. She is very family oriented (I call her Mrs. Inside, while I am like a Mr. Outside, terms used in a sales organization), and felt a new infant would give her the companionship she was not getting from me during this grueling study/flying routine I was heavily into. So, God seems to have blessed us with the "reverse rhythm" process, in that we somehow arrange our love schedules to fit into Nedra's fertile times, such that she can get pregnant easily if she wants to. Thus, "boom", with my very busy schedule, she got pregnant quickly. Nedra's friends often asked her, what with Frank's busy schedule, how could you find the time to get pregnant? Her ready response is "We met at the door on occasion, and Boom, I was pregnant." That's the truth, and that's how it happened.

Once she got pregnant, we were concerned that the bridge across the river between Portsmouth and *Kittery* Maine, the town at the Portsmouth Naval Shipyard (home of the Navy Hospital for the delivery) would be raised for a boat passing, and we would have a baby delivery in the car. We feared that scenario but, PTL it did not happen. As the due date got closer, Nedra wrote her mom and asked for help (again), since her mom Wannie was very close to Nedra and vice versa. Wannie flew in, and was there to help feed and take care of our four youngsters when Nedra made the trip to the Portsmouth Naval Shipyard hospital to deliver our fifth child. The big joke we all remember well about Wannie's arrival and trip involved our daughter Carol. Carol always was our school oriented child, and she told Wannie, after she complained about cost of plane tickets and such for these trips, that Wannie needn't worry about flying home. We had this large tree in our front yard with two large branches in a Y configuration. All we had to do was get a large tire inner tube rubber strap and make the branches into an oversize sling shot and shoot Wannie back to St. Louis for free! Carol of course, had seen the boys sling shots so typical in those days, and saw this as a very practical and cheap way to get Wannie home. We all had a real big laugh over that story, and still do till this day.

Nedra's day now got really close, we began worrying about continuing on for a graduate degree. Well Nedra and I had a long standing "pact" that she seemed to get pregnant at every school I attended in the service. We told ourselves that this was *not* a school assignment, since we were already in AFIT (Air Force Institute of Technology, the term for this assignment) and this was a continuation of our *old* assignment. Well, the Air Force Times newspaper came out next month, and in the assignments section, there we were, Captain Frank D. Szachta was assigned from AFIT to AFIT, another school assignment. Sure enough, now that Nedra was no longer bored, since she had to raise her infant, Frank Jr., we got another school assignment, and she got pregnant again. Once more her friends started asking her, where did you find time to do this since we students were always busy studying or flying all over the country on our few weekends off? Her ready response was "I met him at the door twice" and sure enough, she got pregnant twice. The same worries about the bridge being open at delivery time started up all over again.

As our good luck continued to follow us, March 20, 1965 saw our smooth trip across the Piscattaquay River into Maine, and to the Portsmouth Naval Shipyard hospital, for the on-time delivery of Evelyn Anne, our sixth child. School was going well, and the rocket receiver design I was to do as a practical thesis was completed by another student. It was needed now, and my design classes for transistor circuits were not done yet. Thus, in the next few months my thesis advisor changed mine to render that receiver more reliable, since the first design proved unreliable due to the shaking and vibration present in the Nike Rocket application of the unit.

So, Frank's hands were quite full with his duties and school-related work. Nedra was deftly handling all the household and children obligations. Six children, all of whom remember the grace and patience with which Nedra methodically cooked, cleaned, drove errands, patched scrapes and cuts, lifted up those who were blue, scolded those who "crossed the line," and morally supported her Air Force officer husband. Also, the entire family had become fully accustomed to the transient military life. Soon, the time for school to end drew near, which meant it was nearly time to "move on."

CHAPTER TEN:
PAYING THE PIPER

On July 16, 1945, in the desert in southern New Mexico, the United States detonated the world's first man-made nuclear device. Code named "Trinity," the shot, like the fission/fusion reaction, ignited the paranoid chess match that we all know as the "Cold War." Now that the actual threat of catastrophic destruction and death was real (the war in the Pacific, of course, ended as a direct result of nuclear weaponry), the United States, along with a number of other nations that possessed the potential to develop and deploy such weapons ultimately signed a Limited Test Ban Treaty. The treaty prohibited nuclear explosions that could cause radioactive debris to be present outside the territorial limits of the State under whose jurisdiction or control the explosions were conducted.[22] Because of an atmosphere of distrust amongst the signatories to the treaty—namely the western nations of the United States and Great Britain did not trust the Soviet Union--, and also because the language of the treaty as signed left some "holes" through which a straight-faced government could thread some testing, the idea of Long Range Detection (LRD) became a reality.

Collection and analysis facilities and laboratories were established all over the world in U.S. and British military installations. Presumably, the Soviets also built monitoring stations in its own global strongholds. In September of 1949, using seismic information collected by the U.S. Coast Guard, a number of governmental agencies were called upon to begin assessing whether or not an

---

[22] http://www.state.gov/t/isn/4797.htm

atomic (nuclear) event had occurred, and where. LRD collections provided samplings of the atmosphere to a number of laboratories for analysis, concluding that a nuclear device had been detonated, and not by the United States or the United Kingdom. Eventually, it surfaced that the Soviet Union had detonated its own nuclear device on August 29, 1949, code named "Pervaya Moniya," or "First Lightning."[23]

The Cold War had begun.

Having been the happy recipient of a first-class education, Frank and his family were prepared to embark on the balance of his Air Force career, and the opportunity to put all of that education to good use. It was the summer of 1965 and the Cold War was in full swing, and the Air Force needed Frank's experience with nuclear weapons and current knowledge in engineering. Nedra was just looking forward to being out of the snow!

She writes:

In August of 1965, Frank graduated *Summa Cum Laude* and we were on our way to California—next base, McClellan AFB in Sacramento. Sunshine without snow and all the winter clothes. Seems like, in New England, I spent a lot of time dressing and undressing children with all that cold weather!

Either way, it's obvious the family was excited about

---

[23] A Fifty Year Commemorative History of Long Range Detection; HQ Air Force Tactical Applications Center, Patrick AFB, 1997.

California. Let's have Frank tell us more:

As we were finishing our College assignment from the Air Force Institute of Technology, some of my classmates started getting their next assignments. My closest friend Raoul Barker was a Regular Officer (as compared to my Reserve Officer on extended active duty) received an assignment to a secret outfit called the Air Force Technical Applications Center (abbreviated AFTAC) with a duty station at Thule Air Base on Greenland. Although he went to Washington D.C. for a briefing on the nature of the assignment and would get additional training at a base in Denver, CO. Naturally he was not elated about the remote duty assignment, which meant his wife would stay in Florida with her family while Raoul completed his remote duty assignment.

Raoul and I worked side by side on our Masters of Electrical Engineering and I was disappointed that my assignment was late in arriving. It seemed to us that Raoul's Regular commission status played a role in his getting selected for this elite classified organization. Lo and behold, two weeks later I got a postcard notifying me that I would be assigned to the AFTAC 1155th Technical Operations Squadron (1155th TOS). What a pleasant surprise for us, and a shocker to Raoul and I considering my Reserve Officer status. Raoul groused about this for a few days, but the ways of upper Air Force assignments are a mystery to most of us, and this sure fit the bill there.

I later understood that my good fortune of both having graduated in my BSEE program at the top of the class (thereby qualifying for an invitation to acquire my MSEE) may have been a factor in my being assigned to AFTAC at McClellan AFB. The reason has to do with my thesis, which was focused upon improving the reliability of radio reception inside a Nike missile. Up to that point, the very high (55g) g-forces achieved by the Nike missile would tend to disrupt and render radio communication with the missile inoperative. After reviewing the existing receiver, I discovered that some of the parts of the units were frail and unable to withstand the high g-forces of a Nike missile launch. My thesis involved better, stronger devices for receiving and passing radio impulses inside the IF stages of the receiver. I believe that related-field thesis may have caught the attention of the higher-ups at AFTAC.

I completed my thesis in late August concerning the Reliability Improvements for a Nike Mounted Radio Receiver and had a few weeks to get ready for the long move from Portsmouth, New Hampshire to Sacramento, California. We planned a short leave/vacation stop in St. Louis, Missouri to visit Nedra's family and show them our two youngest children born while I was in college at UNH. The time flew, and soon we packed up our 60 Pontiac Station Wagon as the moving company packed and loaded all our household goods for the cross country move west.

The trip went smoothly once we set up a schedule wherein we would start each days travel early, so we could drive about 100 miles before breakfast. We would drive again and stop around 2 to 3pm so the kids could swim at the motel pool at each stop. Poor Nedra made much of the trip facing backward as she changed diapers on Frank Jr. or

Evelyn every few miles. One good outcome of all the early stops involved the small pools at most motel stops. Once the older four kids jumped or dove off the pool diving board, it was only a stroke or two for them to reach the poolside. Thus their confidence level grew fast, and by our California arrival, the older four kids were good swimmers. The short St. Louis vacation flew by, and we continued our westward drive. About two weeks after we left New Hampshire, we pulled into the McClellan Base Housing Office. Fortunately for us, there was ample base housing available at the North Highlands housing area. The houses were very large duplex units for us company Grade Officers, and we were very lucky to move in right away.

After we settled in, I reported to the 1155th TOS and started by classified briefings about the organization and my job as a project engineer under a Captain Bill Manning who had been in AFTAC for many years. It turned out, that most personnel stationed there have been in many of the unit organizations around the world for many years. This realization made me wonder all the more about how I "lucked out" in getting selected for this sharp organization and this nice location on top if that. Since I was a pilot as an additional duty, I also cleared through the Base Operations Office to find out which aircraft I would fly while stationed at McClellan. They briefed me that I could check out in the U-3 (a Cessna 310, or "Blue Canoe" in AF slang, a small twin engine plane, like the one "Sky King" flew), the C-54 (a DC-4, Douglas 4-engine plane) and a C-118 (a DC-6, Douglas 4-engine pressurized plane). The AFTAC Squadron flew the bigger planes, and I would be an additional crewmember on their flights, to train our Special Equipment Operators (SED's) as needed. The checkout schedule was planned, and my first 4 months were pretty busy as I learned my engineering responsibilities at the TOS as well as the plane checkout process for the three planes I would be flying part-time.

McClellan Air Force Base (1935–2001) is a former United States Air Force base located in the North Highlands area of Sacramento County, 7 miles (11 km) northeast of Sacramento, California. For the vast majority of its operational lifetime, McClellan was a logistics and maintenance facility for a wide variety of military aircraft, equipment and supplies, primarily under the cognizance of the Air Force Logistics Command (AFLC) and later the Air Force Materiel Command (AFMC). The United States Coast Guard previously operated Coast Guard Air Station Sacramento at McClellan AFB as a tenant activity, operating and maintaining several HC-130 Hercules aircraft. CGAS Sacramento continues to operate at McClellan following its closure as an Air Force Base and is the only remaining military aviation unit and installation on the airfield.[24]

The above Wikipedia description is basic, but doesn't come close to telling the entire story. The Air Force Logistics Command, which was a procurement, supply and

---

[24] http://en.wikipedia.org/wiki/McClellan_Air_Force_Base

material command, was earlier merged with the logistics research and development command. In 1950, these commands were split into two separate commands, and the super-secret AFTAC became a Special Reporting Group. The Air Force's west coast center for AFTAC operations was the 1155th TOS at McClellan AFB, just north of Sacramento. The basic mission of AFTAC was to monitor the globe for nuclear events, then to collect and record data from those events and submit them to national authorities and to interested military personnel. Headquartered at Patrick Air Force Base on Florida's east coast, the Air Force Technical Applications Center is the sole Department of Defense agency operating and maintaining a global network of nuclear event detection sensors. This global network is the U. S. Atomic Energy Detection System. Once the USAEDS senses a disturbance underground, underwater, in space or in the atmosphere, AFTAC's laboratories analyze the event for nuclear identification and report the findings to national command authorities through Headquarters, Air Force.[25]

Since the work assignment was classified, I could not tell the family and friends what I was doing, so conversations centered on family and hobbies only. In recent years our organization became a Direct Reporting Unit, and our Mission Statement was declassified. We operated the "Free World's Atomic Energy Detection

[25] http://www.fas.org/irp/agency/aftac/intro.htm

Systems-World-Wide." With the Cold War in full press during these years one could easily see how busy we could be.

The enjoyable aspect of being in such a special outfit was readily apparent in the personnel selected to work in the unit, and the rapid and timely promotions that nearly all personnel enjoyed from being in this professional

----

Organization. One of the nice flying duty assignments came after about a year at McClellan when our Commander, a one star general stationed at our Virginia Headquarters near Washington D.C. scheduled his annual flying trip to our Pacific locations. I was assigned as a third pilot on the aircrew in our C-118 (DC-6) aircraft for this long and arduous trip. The plane flew to the East Coast to pick up the General and his staff, and returned to McClellan to pick up our extra crewmembers. From California, we flew to Hawaii, Pago Pago, New Zealand, three stops in Australia, the Philippine Islands, Korea, Japan, Wake Island, Hawaii, and then home to McClellan again. We stopped at each location for one or two days, and then continued the trip. Since the plane flew at only 240 knots airspeed, you could find that each flight leg was from 8 to 12 hours.

Although we saw many exotic locations one can only dream of, the duration of each stop was too short to really get to know the cultural aspects of the country we were visiting. The purpose of the trip however was for the General and his staff to boost the morale of our personnel working in small groups at our many operating locations. All in all, it was an exciting trip to many unusual locations, and as a pilot I learned a lot about slow flight and navigation over the large expanse of the Pacific Ocean.

After two years at McClellan the organization offered me an assignment as an engineer with an additional duty as an air operations officer at the 1159th TOS at McChord AFB, Tacoma, Washington. My air ops duties would involve some temporary duty (TDY) at Eielson AFB, at Fairbanks, Alaska and additional duties as a base Operations pilot in the C-47 Gooney Bird that I had flown during my college assignment. I would fly the U-3 again as well. Besides those duties I would be an assistant project Officer on several ground systems that the Squadron controlled throughout the western states. My Squadron Commander would be Colonel Mike McMichael who would be a super leader I was to learn later, while my superior would be a Lt. Col. Snipes. It turned out later that I was also an Instructor Pilot again at McChord, as I was during college. This role would create bit of friction; I learned later I would need to give annual check rides to Lt. Col. Snipes, my direct work supervisor.

On the homefront, the children and Nedra were adjusting to California life. The oldest son, Steven, now 61 years old, recalls the transition. Steven had been in middle school in California, where, "...we lived in base housing, although the base was situated a few miles away, so it was like living in the suburbs...it was the first time we had ever encountered Hispanics. In our community, the officers were on one side and the enlisted on the other, and we all went to the same school...it was kind of rough with the Hispanics in the same school as the Air Force kids..."

With three years separating him and the next child, Carol, Steven says flatly that he didn't have much interaction with the others, especially the youngest ones. Steven is slightly built—a runner's body—and his demeanor is that of a man accustomed to facing challenges. Continually scanning his laptop during our interview, he struggles to breathe sometimes as we talk, and tells me about the throat cancer that he defeated four years ago; the cancer that has returned and has him taking a number of medicines with strange-sounding names. Despite all that, Steven strikes me as a guy who, like his father, has never been comfortable with the word, "can't." He does not say so explicitly, but it becomes rather evident to me that growing up with an absentee Dad affected him.

"When we moved to Washington, [Dad] was never home, and I got involved in long-distance running. Mom came to everything; track in the spring, cross-country in the fall, she was there. There might be only ten people at the cross-country meet, and she was one of 'em...Up there, in Washington, they would have the track meets on Friday night, like football in the south, and the stands were packed! Even broadcast them on television..."

Steven recalls one night when his school was hosting an invitational meet, "I can't recall if Dad was there or not, but I won, and the announcer was having trouble pronouncing my name; he called me 'Sanchesta,' or something like that..." Steven distinguished himself as an All-State athlete in high school, and, had the family not moved away from Washington to St. Louis for his senior year, may have taken his career further. (Given the opportunity to spend his senior year in Washington by living with his track coach, the Szachtas declined, a decision that, Steven says, they regretted later in life.) Even so, Steven went on to coach the Hazelwood Central High School track team to the 4A State Championship in 1987, an honor that

Steven says was "like having a baby!"

Steven taught school for 19 years, then left teaching to join with a data center company which is now called River City Internet Group. "I started at the bottom as Tech Support, and now I run the company." This revelation does not surprise me one bit. Also not surprisingly, Steven is driven, loves to work, and is always planning his next move. He's deep into a "rolling restoration" of a 1978 MGB, loves playing golf, and may one day consider joining his father in retirement in Florida. But for now, he's just enjoying the game. "I'm quite good at mergers and acquisitions, buying and selling companies, and acquiring companies in distress," so his company likes having him around.

As far as he and his mother are concerned, there was obviously a very strong bond. "I spoke with my mother every day of her life, 365 days a year I'd call—he'd [Frank] never answer—and we'd talk. I either went to see her or called her on the phone every single day."

"They [his parents] had a very interesting life...they loved to dance and play hard!"

It is worth noting again that a large family in the middle of the Twentieth century where the father is not often in the day to day picture cannot be described as unique. However—and this has to be mentioned—we are just now beginning to see and feel the effects of the absentee dad as the children of those families move into the second half of their own lives. On the outside, these children are quick to speak about this phenomenon using words with forgiving undertones. Acceptance, understanding and resignation are all parts of it. Whether these children have grown up to do

----

things differently remains to be seen. But for the Szachta children, having an incredibly strong force in the person of Nedra went a long way in the direction of compensating for their own absentee dad.

With a scant three years remaining in his Air Force commitment, Frank and the family loaded up and headed out one more time.

I accepted the shift of assignments within AFTAC since the Air Operations job appealed to me, and besides our family had never been in the Northwest before, and this seemed a perfect chance to see that part of our fine country. So in the fall of 1967 we took a leave to visit Nedra's parents in St. Louis once more, and then we drove west again to the green north west corner of the US.

While at McClellan I was blessed (or lucky again?) to get some good efficiency reports that would be needed in a few years when I would become eligible for promotion to Major. When we arrived at McChord AFB, we were given a fine three-bedroom home (no duplex for us here) which was large, modern, and lovely. I settled into my dual role job readily, and the base Ops checkout in the C-47 went smoothly, with an upgrade to Instructor Pilot (IP) right away. I was now only three years away from retirement, but the Viet Nam war was escalating monthly, and as an IP in a C-47, my likelihood of shipping to the war zone loomed ahead. Of course our mission priority was right up there with the war situation, but two years down the road the likelihood of an overseas move became imminent.

After several air operations in Alaska, and many flights checking out new pilots to the base and the annual check flight to Lt. Col. Snipes and many others kept me pretty busy. Most of the Squadron officers played golf on Saturdays, but that luxury was not in the cards for me since the training and support flights kept be busy most week-ends.

There was a tragic accident in 1969 in the C-47. I checked out a new co-pilot Captain on his way to Viet Nam in about 4 flights in one week. The following week there was flight to transport about 15 personnel to a California base, and the Base Weather Officer (a pilot I gave annual check flight for each year) and the new co-pilot I checked out recently was to be the co-pilot on this trip. The first thing I heard was that the plane crashed just after take-off. Since I was the base's first line IP in the plane, several friends from all over the nation called the Squadron to see if I was killed in the crash. It turned out that the right engine lost a ring cam gear, which meant the engine stopped developing any power, and the plane commander tried to turn back to the runway. He was too low, and the plane stalled into the ground, and the crew all died, while the passengers all walked out of the plane unscathed.

They tried to blame the plane's pilot as the primary accident cause, since a tower man said the pilot was making all the radio calls instead of flying the plane. I knew the pilot's voice perfectly, as well as the co-pilots voice since I had just checked him out recently. After about a month they let me listen to the tapes of the accident calls and I confirmed my thoughts about the crash, and the fact that the copilot made all the calls. The Weather Officer's wife was relieved when the primary accident cause was revised to mechanical failure. Another fact that shocked us, was when at the Weather Officer's funeral, his widow told Nedra that it was blessing that her husband was killed since they only had one child, while if it had been me, our six children would be too big a burden for Nedra to bear. This was a true lovely and considerate Air Force wife.

Family life in the military, as we've seen, is something removed from the day to day life of most families, especially in the mid- to late-Twentieth century. Children of career military parents learn early how to be mobile, how to make fast friends, and how to accept change. That's often one of the most difficult obstacles in life, in general. People often become accustomed to the familiar—surroundings, people, climate, etc. As a result, the boundaries that define many peoples' existence tend to be close, their vision, narrow. Not so with military families. Military people have minds that are more receptive to new locales, new types of people, new routines, schools, churches. They become comfortable with the very real fact that while places and faces change, people are people.

One of the major differences within the Szachta family is that the older four children, Steve, Carol, Bob and Jean, were growing up while the Szachtas were actually in the Air Force. For Frankie and Evelyn, their formative years came after Frank retired from the Air Force. Evelyn describes it as having "two families," because by the time she and Frankie were in their teenaged years, the other four were out on their own and Frank had already retired from the Air Force. Evelyn will tell us more about this later.

But I had the opportunity to interview a modern-day Nedra. Her name is Rachel Clark, and she is married to Chief Master Sergeant Charles Clark, who is approaching mandatory retirement after thirty years in the Air Force. "Chuck" and Rachel have been married for years, which means that Chuck had already established himself as a career military man. Rachel knew this going in, and embraced it as Nedra did, albeit with a greater understanding of her future husband's goals and desires.

One other factor of my giving check rides annually to my supervisor came to light one year. Since my promotion to Major was due soon, I made a flight to the Air Force Personnel Center at Randolph AFB, Texas, to review my personnel file. I found out that Lt. Col. Snipe had rated me an 8 overall, while a nine rating would likely be needed for a promotion. Fortunately for me Col. McMichael had upgraded my rating one step, just the needed step to get me a promotion. He basically said in a few words that Snipes rating was unfair, and a real break (Lucky again?) for me. When I got back to the Squadron I thanked Col. Mike for his words and upgrade, and he said," you deserved it", and I was really thankful I had him on my side.

Just like Rachel and Chuck, the Szachtas had mixed feelings about the approaching conclusion to Air Force life. But I doubt Nedra knew this happened:

As my three years at McChord drew near, at the 19 and 1/2 year point of my career, I felt guilty that many friends were being shot at in Viet Nam two and three times, and my name had not been called once yet. I made a discrete inquiry to Randolph AFB, the Personnel HQ and asked about my situation. The assignment Officer was also curious since C-47pilots were in demand. After he looked up my records on the computer, he realized that my AFTAC position had shielded me from their view when reviewing available pilots. Now, he told me, I would be getting called up for a Viet Nam assignment. I asked him if he could send an advance copy of the orders to our squadron so that we would have more time to settle the family if I was to ship overseas. He agreed to that, and shortly Col. Mike called me into his office a few weeks later to tell me of a possible overseas shipment. He wondered how our Squadron heard direct from Randolph instead of via normal channels from AFTAC HQ. I kept quiet, and didn't tell him of my calls to Randolph. Lo and behold (More luck?) my orders were cancelled, since President Nixon had started a wind-down of the war, and any Reserve Officers that would go past their 20 year service date while in Viet Nam, were not allowed to go there at this time. What a blessing, wow.

Shortly my 20-year date of active duty service was approaching.

Nedra's father was getting very ill with cancer, and we started to think about moving the family back to St. Louis, so Nedra could help her mother in this time of need. In addition, we had to think about getting the kids in school before the Sept. school year started. So, in mid-August, we planned a trip to get Nedra and the family to St. Louis. We planned to fly Nedra and the three youngest children to St. Louis, and the three older ones and I would drive there. Nedra had the cat and three kittens with her in a cage on the airliner. The three older kids and I drove our 67 Pontiac Station Wagon for the journey east. Steve our oldest child was already 16, and he could help me drive. We made real good time the first day out of Tacoma, and were already in eastern Colorado. We told Nedra we were east of Denver, but not how far east.

Early the next day we pulled into St. Louis. One thing that helped us save time on this drive was the way Carol kept making baloney sandwiches as Steve and I kept taking turns driving. We still laugh about that fast trip, to this day.

When I first entered the military at the age of 17, the thought of a 20-year career was never on my mind. Twenty years was forever to a teenager! Somehow, a time span of those two decades was always just a segment of life for the Szachtas. And now it was over. No parties. No celebration. No hoop-lah. On to the next. Nedra writes:

Frank retired from the Air Force in January of 1971.

I came back in August the prior year to get the children started in school back in St. Louis. My father was getting quite ill at the time and it seems he was waiting for me to come home, as he knew I would take care of Mom. He died in October and we moved Mom in with us. This was a very traumatic time for me—new neighborhood, no friends, no husband! My mom and I were also good friends so there was no problem there. We rented a house in Maryland Heights for nine months [*how apropos!*]. When Frank returned home after retiring, we began looking for a house to buy.

Frank Szachta entered the Air Force as an entry-level Airman and rose to the commissioned rank of Major, always tested in the highest percentile of his classes, earned his pilot wings and flew a number of different types of aircraft, amassing some 7,300 hours of flying time. He was the co-pilot of the B-47 Stratojet that was America's first line of offense in the Cold War. He also earned a Bachelor's and Master's degrees in Electrical Engineering, became an expert in nuclear warfare, and was hand-picked to work in a highly-classified nuclear monitoring facility. After twenty years as a busy, successful military man, it was time to move on.

Chapter Eleven:
Frank The Civilian

There are a number of ways retired military men respond to no longer being military men. Usually, successful military men (and women) don't want to cozy up to a rocking chair and read. Of course, more time for golf and fishing, traveling, and "giving back" to the homebound spouse, are always attractive options. But those who've been busy usually like to remain so, and even though military retirement pay for officers isn't bad, it's not often enough to support a lifestyle. There is a lot of life after the military, and Frank and Nedra so embarked.

I was hired by the Skydock Division of the St. Louis Car Company in early January of 1971. I actually started working while still on final leave upon retiring from the air Force. My duties involved de-bugging and revising the electrical circuits and systems on movable loading bridges installed at airports so that passengers could easily get on and off modern jets. Within a week, Mr. George Fish the Vice-President of the Skydock Division that hired me, promoted me to be the Project Engineer on the Eastern Airlines Project at JFK airport in New York City. We were installing seven Skydock units at JFK for EAL. We knew that EAL's new VP Frank Borman of Apollo 8/NASA fame was a "Take Charge Leader," and he put a lot of pressure on our company on this project. These loading bridges arrived at JFK in September of '70, and none of them were operational yet. I worked close with Mr. Fish to try to get installation problems under control. We prepared a "Milestone chart" which clearly showed the problems we were having with the installation, and our solutions to correct them. Each of the seven units was covered as well as the 27 problems we identified and our engineering solutions to get them ready for service. We knew Mr. Borman the former astronaut liked such charts and we hoped it impressed him with our diligence. My wife Nedra hoped that after 20 years of extensive travel in my air force career, that my first civilian job would have a relaxed pace with 40 hour work weeks. She hoped we would be a more closely knit family unit. This EAL project had me flying to New York every 2 or 3 weeks, and spending many late night hours on the Skydock problems and the Milestone chart.

By 1971, Steve, Carol and Bob were teenagers, with Jeanne right behind. Frankie and Evelyn were younger, and neither has much recollection of the Air Force. It's obvious that Nedra was hoping for just what Frank described above: a more stable and "close knit" family unit. Frank obviously wanted to do some good with his knowledge and education, and also wanted to do something significant. The EAL Skydock job seemed to be an opportunity that delivered that to him, and although he was satisfied with his choice, he was well-aware of Nedra's disappointment. Nedra, nevertheless, supported her husband as always.

It was quite apparent to us workers at St. Louis Car Division of General Steel Industries that the Rapid Transit Car industry was losing money on each car they produced.

It seemed the big city inspectors from New York and Chicago were tough to please. Thus each car built underwent numerous repairs and paint touch up such that the slim profit margin evaporated. Thus, as the company speeded up production, it meant the losses went faster also. The airport loading bridge division where I worked was smaller by far, but we were also losing money.

Our problems in Skydock Division stemmed from the fact that we inherited an underbid product from a West Coast Company This was coupled with the fact that the entire loading bridge was never assembled as a unit until it was at the airport. On the Eastern Airlines (EAL) units that I was installing at JFK airport in New York city the problem was more serious yet. The NY Iron workers we hired for the bridge assembly were among the highest paid workers in the nation. Coupled with the severe winter we were having in 1971 made our efforts very expensive, to say the least. Since EAL had hired Astronaut Frank Borman of Apollo 8 fame as their new Vice-President, my problems as Project Engineer for the seven EAL Loading Bridges at JFK airport were under closer scrutiny than ever.

With Mr. Fish's making me a project engineer on the EAL/JFK project, the travels resumed again. Not only was there a lot of night homework as I tried to learn the Skydock circuits and systems, but trips to New York started on my 4th day at work.

The NY trips continued about every two weeks with an EAL project engineer visiting our plant in between every trip to read our "Milestone Chart" and verify to the Borman that things were on schedule. The rough winter the New York area was experiencing sure slowed down our work. The Plant in St. Louis was quite antiquated. There were dirt floors in most of the plant, a few steam radiators for heat, and bare light bulbs for lighting. These conditions reflected the 1888 opening of this factory, when their product was horse drawn streetcars for the St. Louis Transit System. Thus their ability to produce modern products in the early 70's was handicapped to say the least.

I was a bit embarrassed by the old plant conditions as compared to my Air Force experience working in electronic shops and aircraft hangars. When Frank Borman visited our plant in early February to meet the Company officers and complain about our schedules in finishing his Skydock project in New York, I was scheduled to demonstrate some modifications we designed and were installing in his units at JFK airport. When I showed our mods to Mr. Borman, he asked me when I joined the company. He was surprised to learn of my Air Force experience and he wished me luck on his project. I later learned that he gave a talk at the Officers luncheon and put pressure on them and the company to finish his project promptly.

It was a few weeks later, near the end of March that Mr. Borman asked Mr. Fish our VP to come to the EAL HQ in Miami for a business visit. Later that afternoon Mr. Fish called the office to tell us that Mr. Borman canceled our Skydock contract as of this date. This was a big shock to the Skydock Team since we felt we were making good progress. My Diary which was a combination business and personal one, had many notes relating to my EAL work. As soon as I heard the bad news from Mr. Fish I wrote in my Diary "Darn him (Mr. Borman) , we were going to finish the EAL Skydocks at JFK on schedule by 21 April as our Milestone Chart showed." Before the afternoon was over, a Mr. Ken Teasdale of a large legal firm in St. Louis visited our offices. He questioned each of us about the EAL and Skydock project about our thoughts on this contract cancellation. When I told him of my diary and the note I wrote the instant I heard from Mr. Fish, he took my diary with him as evidence for the General Steel Corporation It turned out this data was helpful in the case that General

Steel finally won over three years later.

As the St. Louis Car Company a Division of General Steel Industries in St. Louis was struggling to survive, I started a job search again. There were two options I considered after searching the Want Ads several weeks. One job was for a plant manager at INDEECO, the Industrial Electric Equipment Company located in Brentwood, a south St. Louis suburb. My interview with present plant manager —who was being promoted—went well. He was happy with my resume and my past experiences in the Air Force and at St. Louis Car fit the profile of this new job. INDEECO made all sorts of special design electric heaters for industrial applications. The interviewer would be my direct supervisor and our personalities clicked well.

My interview with his boss did not go as well.

He was the company President and a son of the company's owner. He commented on the fact that my degrees from the University of New Hampshire were OK, but that it was not a top notch Ivy League school. As this was a private company, I should have expected this partisan a view, but it upset me nevertheless. Our personalities definitely did not mesh and I feared later clashes if I accepted this job. The trip across town from our home in North St. Louis was not an easy commute either. My thoughts were to decline this job offer.

The second job I considered in my decision to leave St. Louis Car Company was one as a Technical Data Engineer (basically a Technician job) at the McDonnell Douglas Aircraft Company. Smokey Stover, the Flight

Handbook Group Supervisor interviewed me to become the Flight Data Specialist in his Flight Handbook Group. As a former B-47 Co-Pilot, the calculating and revising of a group of aircraft flight performance charts was a fairly easy job. Smokey, the boss's nickname, thought my education overqualified me for this job. He was right, but I looked at this as a chance to enter the huge McDonnell Aircraft Company personnel pool, and to find a promotion in the future. Smokey gave me the job offer. Nedra liked this job offer also since it would offer me a chance for a straight 40 hour work week, with likely no travel requirements. I accepted Smokey's offer and gave St. Louis Car Company my leaving notice.

Two weeks later I started work in the Flight Handbook Group which was located in a company satellite office in the Northwest Shopping Mall just 7 miles west of our home. The Flight Handbook Group was a close knit group of men who had worked with Smokey for many years. I worked hard to learn their routine of Flight Handbook reviews and editorial marking process. We wrote all the military aircraft handbooks for the company which included the F-4 (AF and Navy), F-1 5 (AF) and the vertical takeoff AV8- A (Marines). One immediate problem I noted in the Performance Sections was a blank Part 10 which carried the notation "this page intentionally blank by order of the government" marked on them. When I asked Smokey about this gap he said, "I've been meaning to get around to that section for 15 years." Well, Part 10 was a typical mission profile for each aircraft, and, I guess, Smokey didn't do them due to the rapid turnover in his man writing that part of the handbooks. In reality, all one had to do was build a typical mission profile and use the data from the first 9 parts of the performance data to plan the flight. As a former B-47 pilot, this was what I did for each mission we flew. Anyway, as I learned the procedures of this job, I started to plan a mission for each aircraft handbook as corrections from the aeronautical engineers were being incorporated.

In about three months I completed a draft Part 10 for every aircraft McDonnell produced and Smokey was quite pleased. The tediousness and boredom of this job was rapidly becoming apparent and I found little job opportunities available in the future. The F-15 engineering was near complete, and the F-4 and AV-8 aircraft were well into their development, with no F-18 on the horizon.

By this time, I became involved with neighborhood group on a project to build sidewalks for our grade school children to use for safely getting to school daily. Another engineer friend, Steve Foege of the Olin Brass Company, was helping me on this effort. It took many evenings of effort and it was a relief from the boredom of the handbook job. The sidewalk project later failed, but it was our entry into the local political and social role for Nedra and me. We usually sided with the working groups and in the sidewalk project, and later political activities, we found this placed us in the Democratic circles. Our opposition always seemed to be the Republican groups, who successfully opposed our

- -

sidewalk project, and other rules and laws we saw as needed.

After nearly a year at McDonnell Aircraft Company, I was eager for a change. Nedra could see that I was bored. I even mentioned running for State Representative, to which Nedra replied, "You file, and I'll file," meaning, of course, that if I filed my papers to run for office, she'd file papers of her own: Divorce Papers. How serious she was is known only to her; needless to say, I didn't file.

One day I scanned a want ad in the St. Louis *Dispatch* looking for an Electrical Engineer—that required foreign travel. Although Nedra had her heart set on a husband being home more of the time, the opportunity sounded exciting, and I applied for the job. I discovered that Sverdrup & Parcel was a huge consulting engineering company with projects worldwide. Mr. Allen Baer, the head of the Industrial Groups Engineering section interviewed me in December of 1973. We hit it off very well, and the Algerian oil pipeline project he outlined sounded most appealing. I was hired and gave Smokey notice. He complained that I was leaving too soon, but I told him with part 10 of the Performance Section completed he had a breather until more changes came along. I felt that I had done my part, and he agreed. We parted friends.

It's difficult not to think that Frank was placed on the Skydock job for two reasons: First, if the project could be turned around, the company needed a top-notch take-charge leader, and that's Frank. However, it's possible that

St. Louis Car was already pessimistic regarding the project's success (based upon the obstacles noted by Frank), and slapped a newbie in there to take the fall. Either way, the always optimistic Frank believed in the project, and was disappointed when it fizzled so close to the finish line. We'll see later that a similar event occurred, so one might surmise that Frank was just getting some experience with that kind of a letdown. There is no doubt that the timing of the McDonnell job could have been better, market-wise. However, with the promise of foreign travel and the opportunity to lead a large-scale project, Sverdrup and Parcel was a great choice for this retired Air Force officer.

Chapter Twelve:
Can't Slow Down

*A*fter working at the McDonnell Douglas Aircraft Company for about a year I felt the chances for growth and advancement there were nil. Their new F-15 plane was in production and there were few opportunities for hiring into their engineering groups. One day I read the St. Louis Post Dispatch want ads and saw an interesting ad by the Sverdrup & Parcel Corporation (S&P) for an Electrical Engineer with some overseas travel needed. It sounded just the opposite of my present job at McDonnell Aircraft, with its 40hr work week, and repetitious daily work the norm in the flight handbook group I was in.

I applied for the S & P job and my interview took place at the fourth floor office of Mr. Allen Baer, the Industrial Division Section Head for electrical engineering. I let Mr. Baer do most of the talking and the interview seemed to go quite well that way. He seemed very interested in my work history at the St. Louis Car Division of General Steel Industries. I worked there from Jan 71 through Oct 72 when I went to work for the Aircraft Company The job at the steel Co involved engineering improvements as a project engineer on the Skydock Airport Loading bridges, with a law suit pending against Eastern Airlines for our work at JFK airport in NY City. I vaguely remembered that General Steel hired S&P to be their "Expert Witnesses" in their law case against Eastern Airlines. Anyway, just as our interview was finishing Mr. Baer said "I have someone I want you to meet." He took me into a nearby office of one of his electrical engineers that I recognized at once. He introduced me to Mr. Bill Roa, a very bald professorial looking man and a sr. engineer on his staff. I recall showing Mr. Roa the loading bridges at JFK airport in the spring of 1972. This was just after Mr. Frank Borman, a VP of Eastern Airlines (EAL), cancelled our contract for seven bridges we had been installing there for EAL. It was a bit of "old home week" meeting Mr. Roa and apparently Mr. Baer had been given a favorable report on me because I was hired that morning in late Dec. 1973. I started work there on Dec 26th, 1973.

Sverdrup & Parcel was an American civil engineering company formed in 1928 by Leif J. Sverdrup and his college engineering professor John I. Parcel. The company worked primarily in a specialty field of bridges. The company's headquarters was located in St. Louis, Missouri.

The firm was the designer of the ill-fated I-35W Mississippi River bridge, Minneapolis, Minnesota, 1964 (collapsed on August 1, 2007). The official report by the National Transportation Safety Board blamed the bridge collapse on a design error by the firm, resulting in the gusset plates having inadequate load capacity.

Some other well-known projects of Sverdrup & Parcel include:

- *Amelia Earhart Bridge 1939, Atchison, Kansas*
- *Sidney Lanier Bridge 1956, Brunswick, Georgia*
- *Bridge of the Americas 1962 (also known as Puente de las Américas, Thatcher Ferry Bridge), Panama, crosses the Panama Canal*
- *Chesapeake Bay Bridge-Tunnel, (also known as Lucius J. Kellam, Jr. Bridge-Tunnel) completed in 1964, and named one of the "Seven Engineering Wonders of the Modern World" shortly thereafter.*
- *Busch Memorial Stadium 1966, St. Louis, Missouri*
- *Hearnes Center, 1972, Columbia, Missouri*
- *Puente de Angostura Bolivar, Venezuela, crosses the Orinoco River*
- *Louisiana Superdome, New Orleans, Louisiana, 1975*

Sverdrup & Parcel was succeeded by Sverdrup Civil, which in 1999 was part of the merger between Sverdrup and Jacobs Engineering.[26]

I found out during the interview with Al Baer, that I would be an assistant Group Leader for a Senior engineer, who was having leg pains and could not travel to Algeria, where our job was to design expansion work on an existing oil pipeline. The project included about four trips to Algeria to sketch the present systems and determine their needs for the expansion by: adding pumps at two pumping stations;

---

[26] http://en.wikipedia.org/wiki/Sverdrup_%26_Parcel

adding tanks at the Land Terminal Near the Mediterranean coast; adding two new pump stations; and designing a new Marine Terminal for larger ships. My first task given by Mr. Baer was to learn the project and contract that we were working under for General Electric (GE) International. GE was too busy to do this project so they hired Sverdrup to do it. The contract documents were a stack of books about three feet tall and were made up by about twenty bound books of data. He introduced me to my Group Leader Mr. Al Coffman whose leg ailments caused my hiring to make his foreign trip s for him. The project was called the Sonatrach Oleoduc Project which was French for the Society of Transportation of hydrocarbons via an oil pipeline from Haoud El Hamra about 400 miles south of Skikda at the Mediterranean coast where the oil storage tanks were located. GE was the consortium Lead Team Member that we would be working for. GE wanted this contract since their huge gas turbine engines built at their Schenectady, NY factory to drive the oil pumps. The "Export-Import Bank" financed this project, and we learned this international Bank is primarily financed by US government funds, and in this way US products are used overseas and US jobs are saved. A big lesson in international and now called global commerce. Quite an interesting lesson to learn only after weeks on this new job.

After reading voraciously for a month, I was promoted to Group Leader for this project and started assembling a team of electrical engineers and designers for me to lead on this large industrial project. Mr. Jim Gushaw was the Project Principal (Officer) on the project since he obtained the project from GE, and that's often how project leaders are chosen, I learned. Mr. Gushaw called a meeting of Group Leaders and a study trip to Algeria was discussed and planned. The trip was set for March 1974 and would include all the discipline Group Leaders and Mr. Gushaw so that we could study the present systems and decide the design needs for the: Pipeline Pump Station expansions; the two new pump stations; the new land terminal storage tanks; the new marine terminal; and all the problems associated with interfacing with foreign equipment already there. To say this effort appeared overwhelming would be the understatement of the day.

My work for the first months of the project involved assigning team members Mr. Baer hired to various elements of the project and getting them up to speed on the contract books related to their part of the project. The Sonatrach Leader was a man named Monsieur Fercani and he worked at Sonatrach development which translated into expansion and new projects. As described earlier, if a US firm designed the project to US standards, the products ordered would be US projects. Another facet of international commerce we all learned was the American Petroleum Institute (API) of Houston, Texas set the standards for petroleum projects worldwide. This organization and its standards are the global "bible" in the oil industry. More education for some of us neophytes in the oil industry and large international projects.

Our trip itinerary was a Trans World Airlines (TWA)

flight to Paris, France. After an overnight rest to recover from jet lag, we would leave the next morning on an Air France flight to Constantine, Algeria. The day stop in Paris gave us a brief chance to sight see Paris, which was most enjoyable. My friend Dick Provance knew a little of the French language and he was a good tour guide and helped us select food items from the French menus. The weather was warmer than we had at home and the day in Paris gave us much to enjoy and remember.

The early morning departure came quickly and we went by taxi to Orly Field for the flight south to Algeria. The four-hour flight to Constantine was aboard Air-Inter, the short haul arm of Air France airlines in their two-engine jet transport. Due to the huge crowds of Algerian workers flying to menial jobs in France, GE agreed that our engineers and their team members would fly first class on these flights between France and Algeria. Those these legs of our trips became our favorite since you are treated royally in the first class section, especially on international flights.

The purpose of our first trip was to view and sketch the many systems of the existing facility segments of our discipline (for me that meant the electrical gear and elements) and determine the best way to interface this equipment with the new systems we were going to provide. The weather in Algeria was much, much warmer than our St. Louis weather, and our suits and ties sure seemed out of place in this North African country. The auto drive from Constantine to Skikda at the Med. coast was about 40 miles over narrow, two lane mountain roads. Skikda used to be called Phillipeville a few years before the Algerian revolution sent the French colonists home. This was part of the animosity the Algerians felt toward us westerners. This harsh attitude also came from their socialistic attitudes taken from the Communist nations that supported their revolution.

The drive to Skikda was pleasant but tedious in the sunny daytime hours, but it could turn rough and dangerous on a dark rainy night or a foggy morning. We spent the first days visit with Mon. Fercani and started some short visits around the tank farm and it's control room at Skikda. The Algerians won their revolution about ten years before, and they nationalized the oil industry about eight years ago. In all our dealing, the French language was used in meetings, and the contract basis would be French. This of course would create many problems for us early on since some of our translators in St. Louis were college students, with little engineering knowledge. They translated, for example, a *station shutoff valve* into a *guardhouse*. A funny embarrassment and, although our learning curve was steep, we learned to recover from such mistakes quickly.

A less humorous example of the cultural and international divide occurred soon. After our first day in Algeria, Mr. Jim Gushaw got a message that there was a meeting in NY with GE that he and Mon. Fercani must attend. They made fast reservations to leave the next day and Jim advised our team that Mr. Narayen Bodapati a Project Planner would become our trip leader since he had to leave for NY. Our Senior Sonatrach Engineer tagged by Mon. Fercani to lead us in our inspections was away in Algiers about 60 miles west and that he would join us the following day. In the meantime, lower level Sonatrach employees were tasked to help us find some "as built" drawings we needed and escorted us around the land terminal, as we called this tank farm. The next day as our Sonatrach Leader arrived from Algiers, we had drawings spread all over the desks in his office, and he was really upset. It was a big cultural and political glitch and I apologized profusely for not getting his permission to use his office while he was away. It was not easy getting his cooperation for the rest of our trip, but our honesty and his good command of the English language helped us over this hurdle before long.

The rest of our Land Terminal visit went well and we started planning our drive south to visit the pumping stations leading to the oil pipeline origin at the oil field zone at Haoud El Hamra, Algeria at the north edge of the Sahara desert. As we finished our visit at Pump Station #3 halfway down the pipeline, Mr. Bodapati our trip leader had to return to St. Louis, per Jim Gushaws directives. By default (don't ask me how) I became the trip leader. There were some disagreements developing between two mechanical engineers on the trip named Al Carson and Andy Olizarowski. Al was younger and from our Tucson, AZ office and he was along since he was going to be our field engineer at the pump stations during the construction phase.

The older engineer, Andy was a Polish immigrant US citizen who was to be a design mechanical engineer at our St. Louis Office. I did my best to keep their disagreements under control and kept them from degenerating into fisticuffs. We had young Algerian College students as translators and drivers, and I tried to keep these fellows cool in front of our foreign drivers. They were shocked that two well educated engineers couldn't be more civil on such a trip. They seemed awful immature to me in their behavior but I blamed it on the stress and pressures we were experiencing in this foreign and unfriendly country. Several times in these days we were threatened by security guards at these oil facilities, and the tension was very obvious. My military background and past life experiences prepared me well for such situations, and I felt in control and was enjoying the adventure of this whole trip.

An interesting and funny event happened while traveling south through a small town. We stopped for lunch and our Algerian College student driver/translators asked us what we would like for lunch. The restaurant was a small place with no menus or English spoken either. We saw some cooked chicken and asked for chicken sandwiches. The translators asked us how you make such a sandwich, and we explained that you take two pieces of sliced bread and put some chicken between them. Well, we were surprised when they delivered our lunch to the table. The sandwiches consisted of half of a chicken (bones and all) placed between two pieces of bread. We ate them separately and enjoyed our meal. We later explained the idea of a chicken sandwich in more detail to our translators, and we all had a nice laugh over this meal.

The young translators enjoyed this trip since it was their first exposure to Americans, and our direct and positive cheerful style. They later compared us to their French Consultants from Sonelgaz, the company helping Sonatrach review our design and construction work. They appreciated our friendlier ways and our informal style of working together. One interesting aspect was the fact that our two mechanical engineers arguments were observed by these students. They couldn't understand how two professional engineers from a top notch US company could behave in such a way. I couldn't explain it very well, except to tell them it was a personality clash, and they accepted this. Later I had to give this same explanation to a Mr. Bill Rivers, the President of S&P, when he heard of this problem after our return from the trip.   \

Our drive back to Constantine went smoothly, and the mountain scenery was lovely. There one small mountain I wanted to climb one day. The first Class flight back to Paris was smooth and relaxing after the tense two weeks just experienced. The free first class cocktail was a pleasant respite. We sure were glad GE arranged it this way. Our original plans called for 3 or 4 trips to Algeria during the project; we had no idea that the Algerians and Sonelgaz would force GE to expand this to over thirty trips over the next five years to this relatively unfriendly country. Quite an exciting way to start my career at S & P.

One can only surmise that life back home was progressing as it always had. By 1973, the older children were venturing out on their own. Frankie was in the midst of his substance issues, "while Dad was away,"; Steve was married; Carol was finishing school; Jeannie was married to her boyfriend while attending classes at the University of Missouri as an Art major. Her husband, Dennis, was a music major at the same college, a development of which the family was very appreciative. Bob was already married and working at UPS; and Evelyn was a teenage girl who thrived in theatrical endeavors at school, singing and acting in school plays. Nedra—to vastly understate the situation—

was busy. Yet, the more I interviewed people who knew her, two words were repeated, and often: Elegance and Grace. Because of the proximity of my shop to where Frank lives, and lived, with Nedra for over twenty years, even those who've not been formally interviewed for this book render nearly identical comments. From Peg O'Sullivan to Bill Hall to Mary Kimberlin—going back in time. Nedra, the egalitarian, Nedra the "neighborhood mom," Nedra, the one with the "contagious laughter." Nedra, who believed that "everyone has his or her own way of being wonderful." Nedra the one who made blankets for the vets, fashionable outfits and clever crafts—all while raising an eclectic brood with her husband in absentia.

Our design work continued at full speed over the next years, and my Air Force experience and the new engineers on my team responded to the pressures and deadlines very well. Although the Civil engineers usually lead the project progress but they were behind schedule. To satisfy the clients the project manager asked us, his electrical team to rush ahead and produce some lighting and related drawings so that we could deliver some S & P drawings for client review. For the earliest three trips there were electrical drawings to review, and the Sonelgaz consultants accepted then for review with few questions.

A sad event occurred in the fifth month of the project when a limp noticed in Project Principal Jim Gushaw's walk got worse. He thought it was from a tennis fall but it turned out to be a serious cancer of the bone, and he died within a month. Mr. Lieu Smith became the new Project Leader, and he quickly surmised the need for many more overseas trips due to client demands. He rapidly negotiated a new contract with GE to allow for cost reimbursable trips of an undefined amount, which turned a losing project into a huge cost plus project for S & P. A great team addition came at this time when Lieu brought on board an assistant named Tom Elgin as his project assistant. Tom and I really hit it off, and became close friends for the rest of my time at S & P. Tom was a straight shooter who enjoyed smoking and a cocktail as we left Algeria, and in my mind a perfect friend. Lieu Smith on the other hand was a convert to Mormonism, had quit smoking and drinking, and looked on us as less than good troops because of our enjoyment patterns. He never put any of his subordinates in for company stock, which to us workers represented a downside to his leadership style. He was well organized, and had a trap door memory, so he was good in that respect. Later in the project, Tom became the Project Manager and I was elevated to become his assistant, a nice arrangement for both of us. We had many good times during my 30 trips to Algeria and Tom's 35 trips.

This was huge and profitable project for S&P.

There were some very tense trips in 1979 as Franco, the Leader of Spain, donated Spanish Sahara to Mauritania and Morocco. Algeria protested since they wanted a path through Spanish Sahara to the Atlantic. They had a mining town at Tindhouf that needed water transport for economic reasons. The US was friends with Moroccan Leadership, and they felt if Algeria got an Atlantic port, Russia would use it to service submarines there. So the US sided with Morocco, and Algeria and Morocco started a small-scale war over this border dispute.

Tanks were rolling all over Algeria, and traffic stops were made at each town. Things were very tense at each stop as the military searched Americans very closely, with weapons in our car windows. Several S & P engineers refused travel to Algeria for a time because of this tension, as well as the poor water and sanitary conditions in Constantine and other small towns. Since the French left Algeria after the Revolution, the Algerians were severely undermanned in the technical fields, and the Constantine water system was a typical example of major problems they were facing. There was running water only in the morning and evening for about an hour each time. These conditions lead to cholera outbreaks, bad conditions to say the least. Several engineers got ill on trips, and refused to return to Algeria. All these factors added up to many project delays, and the trips kept adding up.

This was hard on Nedra, to say the least. Every three weeks I would be off to Algeria again. We always traveled on weekends and that meant more time away from the family and more burdens for her to carry. She had to take care of our six children, the home, the cars, and the many problems that growing teen-agers can create. She had several stress attacks during this long travel period, and the rough time she had was immeasurable. It wasn't long after this project that I felt the workload she bore was greater by far than mine was. At that time, after 44 years of marriage, I promised her more help in the kitchen and around the home, and she well deserved that help and more. I got many of the "hero's" pats on the back from my work projects, but in our hearts, many of these awards belong to Nedra.

CHAPTER THIRTEEN:
LOST IN SPACE

*V*andenberg *Air Force Base is a United States Air Force Base located 9.2 miles (14.8 km) northwest of Lompoc, California. It is under the jurisdiction of the 30th Space Wing, Air Force Space Command (AFSPC).*

Vandenberg AFB is a Department of Defense space and missile testing base, with a mission of placing satellites into polar orbit from the West Coast using expendable boosters (Pegasus, Taurus, Minotaur, Atlas V, Delta IV and now SpaceX's Falcon). Wing personnel also support the Service's LGM-30G Minuteman III Intercontinental Ballistic Missile Force Development Evaluation program.

In addition to its military mission, the base also leases launch pad facilities to SpaceX (SLC-4E), as well as

100 acres (40 ha) leased to the California Spaceport in 1995. The base is named in honor of former Air Force Chief of Staff General Hoyt S. Vandenberg.

The host unit at Vandenberg AFB is the 30th Space Wing. The 30th SW is home to the Western Range, manages Department of Defense space and missile testing, and places satellites into near-polar orbits from the West Coast. Wing personnel also support the Air Force's Minuteman III Intercontinental Ballistic Missile Force Development Test and Evaluation program. The Western Range begins at the coastal boundaries of Vandenberg and extends westward from the California coast to the Western Pacific, including sites in Hawaii. Operations involve dozens of federal and commercial interests.

The wing is organized into operations, launch, mission support and medical groups, along with several directly assigned staff agencies[27].

In 1977, the Sonatrache Oil Pipeline Project for GE Intl. was winding down, and a new project was bid and won by Sverdrup. We were selected by the USAF and the Army Corps of Engineers to design changes to a West Coast Space Shuttle Launch Site at Vandenburg AFB (VAFB), CA, near Lompoc and Anna Maria, CA towns. The old site called Space Launch Complex 6 (SLC-6) at VAFB was originally designed to launch a Military Orbital Laboratory (MOL) project in the late 60's. There was little public support to

---

[27] http://en.wikipedia.org/wiki/Vandenberg_Air_Force_Base

move the military into a Space War footing, and that project was closed after SLC-6 was just completed.

The USAF launches most of their military hardware missiles from VAFB in order to attain a polar orbit, so necessary to view the entire globe, whereas the Kennedy Launches from FL only view the middle 2/3's of the globe. This site will use much of the MOL site hardware, which consists of tall (16 story) steel buildings that roll or rails to and from the Launch pad to build up the launch vehicles. At Kennedy, the Space Shuttle is assembled in the huge Vertical Assembly Building (VAB) and then move to the launch pad via a slow moving tractor and launch pad assembly. At VAFB, we must design changes to the existing moving structures to handle the Space Shuttle erection, build-up of the solid rocket boosters, erection and mating of the large External Tank, and finally installation of the payloads into the Shuttle payload bay. In addition, the buildings must all be strengthened to withstand use overpressure loads during the launch period. The shuttle launch blast pressures greatly exceed those of the zMOL project of years ago.

I was selected by Lew Smith, out Project manager of the Algerian pipeline project to be the Electrical Group Leader on the VAFB project. He is the project manager of this huge project also. Since he is a structural engineer, and the structural challenges of the VAFB are the biggest efforts involved in this project, he and many friends in the Special Structural Division are key players on this project.

The biggest factor in this effort became the huge meetings that were held once the project got underway.

With the USAF client, the Corps of Engineers, Govt. manager, and site constructors, as well as all the discipline sections of Sverdrup and Sverdrup Technology of Tullahoma, TN also involved, meetings of 50 persons were common. Since I was having a hard time understanding all the conversations and questions for the electrical section, I got a hearing test and, ultimately, hearing aids. Several friends asked if I wasn't getting to be an "old geezer," but I realized that if I needed them to hear at the meetings, I would use them.

One nice feature of this project was that the Oryalls, our old OCS friends are in the missile Wing at VAFB were there too, and we planned to visit them as site trips developed. As time went on, we did get to visit and stay with the Oryalls on two visits. Nedra accompanied me on these visits, and we had a lovely time getting reacquainted with Orland and Betty Oryall and some of their children home from school. Orland was a regular USAF officer, while I was only a reserve officer. He was promoted to Lieutenant Colonel, and really enjoyed his job on the missile Wing at VAFB. Betty and Orland were catholic like us, and we had many things in common, like large families, and our AF careers. Orland wore glasses even in OCS, so he never was into a flying career, but his specialty was missile defense, and later missile weather launches.

As the project grew, our electrical team got as large as 30 or so, and it was a chore keeping up with the design of all the facility electrical needs. One aspect of the project that I had a problem with involved the Cathodic Protection (CP) elements of much large steel piping that ran underground throughout the site. Since Sverdrup was not well qualified in this field, we hired a specialist consultant for the sire CP survey. Later it turned out, that I did not pick up on one of his recommendations, and an extra charge to the company was made by the Corps of Engineers to correct this deficiency. It turned out that a peer friend named Dan Amsden took my side in this case, in helping resolve the issue. I really appreciated his work in getting me out of this potential jam.

The size of this project, and having to manage the many facets of work going full blast for years on end, was an overtime effort, similar to the Algerian Oil Pipeline. In much later years, I realized what a huge burden these projects put on Nedra in raising the children single handedly. I would remember many a night when I was tired from a full day, and I would go to sleep so I could get up early for work the next day, and Nedra would patiently await our high school children, as they recounted their days activities. In addition, she would share their problems, with friends, and classmates, many a night. Over and over, these burdens were taken over by her, with nary a complaint or question. She was, and is a consummate supermom in all respects. I could never repay her for these many, many long nights and days of turmoil, and elation that our large family of children showered down on her. In later years (1992 or so) I offered to help her (on the basis of this huge guilt trip I felt for not helping her raise the youngsters) in the kitchen, which she rapidly accepted. I now feel the burden (a lot easier than she had) of trying to handle these several jobs, and it's not easy.

As the Space Shuttle Project at VAFB and SLC-6

neared completion of construction, Sverdrup was awarded the "Grand Conceptor Award" mainly on the merits of the complex steel structures completed. Ironically, as the 95% mark was achieved in construction, I was sitting at my desk and got a call from a media person in NY city. He asked me what I thought about the explosion that occurred at Kennedy Space Center one-half hour ago? I was shocked in hearing of the Challenger shuttle explosion, and could only answer, that I was\ only involved in shuttle launch facilities and not the shuttle vehicle, and quietly hang up on the call. This tragedy placed a large burden on NASA to review and improve shuttle safety, and ended any hopes the USAF had to use the shuttle for military launches at VAFB. Sadly, this ended our VAFB project at near its completion date, never to be used for it's designed function.

To me, one of the most transparent issues about Frank's absences is how he describes his eventual understanding and empathy for what his wife had been doing for him and the family for so many years. It might be difficult for a contemporary mind to grasp that Frank, with his brilliant mind, would not fathom the depth and breadth of the task he passively asked Nedra to perform. I mean, how could it be that he could be imperceptive or, far worse, insensitive, to the burden placed upon Nedra? He obviously was aware of the challenges facing each of his children, such as they were. But looking at the man more carefully, one can see the level of focus that was both necessary and achieved as Frank accepted the challenges both in the Air Force and afterward. Additionally—and this is not

----

supported by any overt evidence—it's entirely possible that Nedra either downplayed or, perhaps more to the point, simply excelled at juggling her duties such that her demeanor and the outward appearance illustrated that Nedra "had everything under control." Also, and this is substantiated, Nedra never wanted to do or say anything that may tend to interfere with her husband faithfully and excellently carrying out his duties. Either way, it is comforting to note that Frank eventually found some personal illumination, and gratitude, for his Nedra.

Evelyn, the Szachta's youngest child, now 50 years old, remembers her father somewhat differently than her older siblings (except for Frankie, who is just a year and a half older). Evelyn's earliest memories commence after Frank retired from the Air Force. She recalls a dad who "left the house at 6AM and came home at 6PM," a man who was "phenomenal," who "worked hard" at St. Louis Car Company and then at Sverdrup & Parcel. Evelyn, who is married some 25 years now and makes her home in the rural area outside of St. Louis with her three children, her husband, Steve, and their menagerie of animals including goats, chickens, bunnies and a pair of dogs, calls the family she grew up in the "second family." Speaking of her parents, she says, "I think it was the combination of their personalities, taking the positive aspects of their individual personalities and, having no one else to turn to, they were kind of living the adventure." Evelyn says that the "nomadic personality of my dad thrives on that jetset lifestyle, and my mom got to live that sort of vicariously through him. She got to be the officer's wife, living the cosmopolitan life, as far as she was concerned. It made her feel important, and they were a great team."

I get that. Envisioning how these two people brought their individual talents and skills to the table, and how those meshed, is at the very heart of how this worked. If you recall, Frank just "knew" there was something different about Nedra, and she felt the same. Nedra's sixth sense or intuition or however it is described just knew. Evelyn is just one of the products of that union, and she describes herself as a combination of the two of her parents (as Bob did also). She says, "I'm a lot like my Dad, I have a lot of his DNA, and I'm proud of it. I'm a ridiculously hard worker, and I have more confidence than I should." Yep, that sounds like Frank! "But what I love most about him is his modesty, and he's so excited about life."

Evelyn remembers when she was a girl of eight or so, after Steve and Carol had left, and Bob was pretty much on his own, while Jeanne was at home but in high school with all the demands from that, that she and her father would go out and walk around the neighborhood. "Together, we would hold hands and march in time and sometimes have to do that stutter-step to get back in time, while Dad pointed out the constellations and we sang, 'You Are My Sunshine'...I don't remember the twelve hours he was gone each day; I remember the twenty-minute walk together."

Regarding her mother, Evelyn believes that her own life as a mother, and any success she has with that, is entirely attributable to Nedra. "The best thing she did as a mother herself is support and encourage us with words of praise at our mothering. "She was not a yeller; she was a quiet listener."Evelyn acknowledges that her mom was likely very skilled at mothering by the time Evelyn came along, and that she had likely already made all of her mistakes "with the others!"

Regarding the "others," Evelyn admits, with some resignation, that the family is "fragmented." Obviously, when children grow up and go their separate ways, having and raising families, engaged in their various occupations, friends and hobbies, the result can have an impact upon the core group of people one had in childhood called a "family." Nedra's passing may have contributed to some of that, however, as Evelyn notes that, for example, Jeannie enjoyed a close relationship with her mother for years. This evolution is something that Frank feared. Knowing that Nedra was the "hub" of the family, Frank worried that the family may fragment further after her passing. He has worked hard to do what he could to maintain the family foundation, to keep the siblings in touch with one another. But his quiet strength, based upon an immense faith, has allowed him to recall his individual ability to accept that which he cannot change.

CHAPTER FOURTEEN:
TAKING THE WIFE ABROAD

I was between projects at Svedrup & Parcel in St. Louis and the Section Manager, Dan Amsden gave me several small projects as they came into the Electrical Section of the Industrial Division. One day in late '85 he told me that the Architectural Section of the Buildings Division in the building across the street had picked up a huge Defense Project for the USAF. Eventually after the USAF accepted the project, they would hand over the key (as in a turnkey project) to the Royal Saudi Air Force, since the project was an Air Defense Command infrastructure , commonly called the "brick and mortar phase" of the project, throughout the Saudi Kingdom. It was called the Peace Shield project. Their project manager asked our division for a short term assist in the design of a central control room to manage the operation of a small complex of buildings. They estimated this assistance would require about 4 weeks of a system control design effort. Since I was temporarily out of work, and my Air Force background seemed to fit the project needs, Dan asked me to work across the street with the Peace Shield team for the next month or so. Thus I began working with the architecture crew on Peace Shield in the 801 11th street building. \

I first met and introduced myself to Ken Schaefer, an architect, and the project manager for Peace shield. I related my Air Force background to him, and my recent experience on an Air Force project during our redesign of the space shuttle launch site at Vandenburg AFB, CA. He was satisfied that I would be capable of designing the control room they were seeking help on, and I started to meet the rest of the electrical and mechanical sections of their design team. Ken briefed me of the general aspects of the Peace Shield project. The entire project was approved by a LOU, which is a Letter of Understanding between the Saudi Government and the US government, for the design and construction of the infrastructure of an Air Defense Command System for the Saudi Kingdom. It would consist of the remodeling of an underground Command Center in Riyadh, five more sector command centers underground in sections of the country, and 18 Long Range Radar sites around the country perimeter and up the center spine of the nation. Although not classified, we were briefed that the nature of the project was considered confidential, and not to be discussed outside the company. The USAF was to be the design team leader. They then contracted with a consortium of firms, CRSS & Metcalf & Eddy consulting firms of Houston, Texas was to oversee our design, and then to run the construction effort in Saudi Arabia. S & P would also have an oversight team in Saudi to ensure for the USAF, that the construction followed the design correctly. The Saudi's gave the USAF full latitude in their design needs, and funded the entire project with one check to the US government for $3 Billion dollars. It was a huge project, and a good opportunity for Sverdrup to make some nice profits. Since the USAF was the overall design leader on the project, I felt well suited for the design task Ken asked me to perform. The second day on the project, some CRSS staff members were coming to St. Louis today, and I was asked to sit in on the meeting. After a brief reading of the project requirements for the control room needs, I felt ready for the meeting with the CRSS and USAF project members. The group meeting turned out to be a huge gathering, and I sat in the back of the room. I spoke very briefly when the LRR control room was discussed, and listened and learned a lot during the meeting. Part way through the meeting the subject of "Standardization" came up and my ears perked up. This term is very common in the USAF, and as a former bomber crewmember in the Strategic Air Command, I was very familiar with its meaning and usage. A CRSS man named Carter Rohan was speaking their team leader for standardization. I waited for an opening and then told of my experience in the USAF with standardization during my air force career. Carter asked to meet with me later, and our project manager Ken Schafer concurred. Carter and I left the big meeting for a separate small meeting in another room, as the general conference continued. Carter gave me his ideas on the USAF needs for standardization on the six command centers as well as the 18 LRR's, and we became friends at once.

Carter and I agreed to write up our ideas on the project standardization needs, and I had just coordinated with the client for an expansion of my needs on this project. After discussions with Ken our project manager, we agreed that my standardization work with Carter would be added to my control room design effort. I told Dan, my Section manager of this added work and he was pleased since our Division work load was slow at this time.

After about a week's work on the control room design I talked to Nedra and we decided to think about a grand finale project with the company Since I was just over 55 years of age, the thought of early retirement started to cross my mind. Moreover, Nedra had never been overseas yet, and I thought that this would be a good chance to accomplish this goal.

Nedra initially was very much against leaving St. Louis for years. She was a mother and grandmother through and through and the thought of leaving them for a year at a time did not appeal to her. I mentioned that we started out alone together over 35 years earlier, and the adventure of this project was worth considering. Finally, I thought of a perk that may help convince her. I told her "We will be making a good salary, and that if a child or grandchild got ill, she could fly home at once. In fact I told her she could come home as often as she felt necessary. She didn't have my tax restrictions of 35 days a year at home as a maximum. This offer seemed OK to her, and I prepared a half-page, handwritten resume volunteering for the Saudi Assignment on the Peace Shield Team f or Mr. Ralph Beil, the project executive.

To my surprise, Mr. Beil called me into his office the next day and offered me the job of Saudi Project Leader for the Sverdrup Team. This was more than I expected, since I didn't know the Saudi language or other factors were needed, and I soon got cold feet about the offer. I talked with Mr. Beil at length a few days later and expressed my apprehension to accept his offer. He saw my position and said that the President had talked with a company architect named Gregory Khaklos, working in Singapore, and that Greg accepted the offer to be the Team Leader. Mr. Beil than surprised me again by offering me the job of Assistant-Team Manager and Lead Electrical on Peace Shield in Saudi. After more chats with Nedra, I accepted the offer. The next step involved getting transferred from the Industrial to the Buildings Division so that I could become a full time Peace Shield engineer.

During our stateside design efforts, we made friends with the Buildings Division engineers as well as foreign engineers from our Saudi partners engineers. In the Kingdom of Saudi Arabia, any foreign company working there must have a Saudi firm as a partner. Our partner was the Abalkhail Consulting Engineering Company I met Mr. Abalkhail, the president of our Saudi sponsor company, later in the job. He was a University of Oregon educated civil engineer, and a very talented fellow. His engineers working in St. Louis with us were from Ireland (Abalkhail had a Dublin office), Pakistan, Bangladesh, Philippine, Saudis' and others. Quite an international team we were now working with. The percentage of team members was to about 80/20 Americans during our US design work, and

20/80 Americans during our Saudi construction over sight work. The Irish engineers were by far the most capable of the Abalkhail team with the Pakistani and Phillipino men next in line. We had a lady engineer leading our civil engineering of the Long Range Radar sites (LRR) and this would create a problem later. When field work was needed during the design effort, engineers were sent to Saudi Arabia. The Saudi nation treats women the way the US did in the colonial expansion days, that is, women raise children and care for the family home. They do not drive cars or carry on public careers the way ours do in the 1980's. Because of this fact, our lady civil group leader could never make a Saudi field trip.

The irony of Frank's observations in Saudi Arabia as they relate to the treatment of women during American Colonial Expansion cannot go without comment. That is, "women raise children and care for the family home," precisely what Frank asked Nedra to do! Obviously, the difference is that Nedra had a choice; Saudi women did not, and, sadly, still do not.

Here's Nedra's side of that story:

After our last son was married, Frank convinced me to go to Saudi Arabia with him. It was hard for me to leave the children and grandchildren, but the Saudi experience was something I shall never forget. The exotic areas we travelled to, the hardships in other countries…all the different people, dress, languages. It all made me realize how fortunate we all are to live in the USA with all our freedoms.

Our "church" in Riyadh was "underground;" we met in each other's homes. The communion hosts were all consecrated by a priest who would occasionally slip into the country. We would all take turns with the readings—so many foreign accents—all Catholic, all caring for each other. It was beautiful—but scary in case we were caught. It was a growing experience and I became more comfortable with it as time went on. We spent 3 1/2 years in Riyadh and I was evacuated when Saddam invaded Kuwait on August 7, 1990. We didn't know if he was coming right on into Saudi Arabia. Frank had to stay until October 1 to finish his contract. I was a frightening time for all of us!

Nevertheless, I think everyone should live in a foreign country for a while.

Frank continues:

I arrived in Saudi in the Spring of 1987, and Greg drove me to the AT&T housing compound where Nedra and I had a leased villa. The compound had a guarded gate which yielded a nice, safe feeling. The villa was on a small cul-de-sac, a typical three bedroom, one bath home, with central air as one would see in any US subdivision. The compound had a high stone wall all around which added to the secure feeling of the place.

The next day Greg picked me up so that I could start thru security at the Riyadh Air Base, and other arrival formalities. We started the day by meeting the Riyadh

Sverdrup/Abalkhail (AB) team. My assistant was a short Pakistani Electrical engineer. All the other team members were very friendly, and our meeting them went smoothly. Greg liked my friendly and easy going style and used me as his social program director and team leader with most of our team members.

The compound had two nice swim pools, of which I preferred the larger family pool over the smaller heated pool near the bachelor quarters. My daily work routine came to include a short swim every morning before work. I really enjoyed the hot weather and the low humidity made it more comfortable.

Soon I was making friends in the compound with our neighbors. One family in particular was the Bob and Sandy Postma family. Bob was the Vice-President of WESA, which is Western Electric of Saudi Arabia. Bob was a very nice fellow, and our meetings were social as well as business in nature through my association in the Society of Military Engineers (SAME). This multi-national organization was headed by the AF Commander of the Peace Shield project. Greg appreciated me getting involved with this organization since it offered us the chance to stay on a good footing with our Air Force project engineers. It also gave us a chance to enter and have dinner meetings in some of the exclusive Saudi buildings and organizations all over the Riyadh area.

The King Faisal Hospital (KFH) was reserved for Saudi Royalty, and I heard from my Barnes hospital pheresis nurses that KFH needed pheresis donors badly. When I went there one morning I was told it would be a long wait to get on their pheresis list. When I told them of my pheresis experience and the double level of my platelet output, they started me donating that day. In Saudi, they have a hard time getting blood donors since Saudis' seem afraid of the process, so the expatriate work force supplies most of their donors. They get added donors by forcing drivers license applicants to donate a pint of blood. They also pay $65 for a pint blood donation and $125 for a pheresis donation. From then on I donated pheresis platelets monthly and added some money to it and sent it to the Crossroads Drug Abuse Program of St. Louis. Our son, Frank, is the program director after the program helped him over a problem over ten years before.

The project was running smoothly, and Frank and Nedra were enjoying the time together—and apart, for Nedra made 11 trips home during the time in Saudi. The saying around our friends was "Nedra is the lady who goes home to the US for lunch." Alas, there came a time in the autumn of 1990 when plans changed.

As Saddam Hussein of Iraq invaded Kuwait on Aug 9th or so, it was an earthquake event for all of us in Saudi Arabia. What we considered the most secure country in the Middle East due to their strict rules and ever present police forces of all kinds became overnight the most insecure. The reasons for this were many. Their newspapers didn't even mention the invasion of Kuwait for days. Since we all had the Defense Dept. Armed Forces TV and radio, we all knew instantly via CNN TV of the invasion and its hourly progress. Within 24 hours, the daily hand-off of such TV broadcasts went on as usual and the citizens became outraged by the censorship of the monarchy controlled TV, newspapers, radio, and all media.

Within 2 days, the media became free flowing, and as the pendulum swings, it became unusually gruesome. One article read, :"If birds are falling from the sky, and cars out front are crashing, do not let your husband into the house, since he may have been exposed to a gas attack, and opening the door will expose and kill you too." Of course, this is Mid-East fatality thinking, and quite opposite of the first days censorship.

Since many unit leaders were on vacation in August (typical of European theater) most organizations were being led by their second in charge. This was true of our EDC Team (I was in charge, since Manager Greg Khaklos was on a vacation) as well as our Saudi Partner Mr. Abalkhail was in charge since the President and owner of his company was also on vacation.

Being of a military mind, I started to make out a telephone tree system for communications contact with all our EDC Team members. I fully thought that Saddam would turn right after he reached the Persian Gulf and head for Dhahran, the Saudi Oil zone. I also expected Scud Missiles to be aimed toward Riyadh, the capital city, to damage the Saudi Military forces, and the Monarchy.

Since 2/3 of the EDC Team members were Abalkhail employees, I had to brief my counter part of their firm, of my plans for our EDC Team and his employees in it. Since we were working at the Riyadh Air Base, I expected this would be a Scud Target zone, and planned to relocate if needed to some old warehouse nearby. I briefed a typically shy and reserved Saudi of my plans, and he was impressed with my military thinking, and the plans for his people. He said "anything you feel you must do, please do it, since we Saudi's were never exposed to such a wartime situation," and were pleased that we would take care of his people in the best way we knew. I was pleased with his support, and the Team members were satisfied that we would work to keep them informed of needs to move or whatever it took to stay safe.

Within days of the invasion, Secretary of Defense Dick Cheney flew over to brief the King of the invasion and the US planned response to help Saudi Arabia repel any possible invasion of their nation. We all were aware of the Saudi penchant for procrastination in such big decisions. It was our long held knowledge that they would let others make the timely decision and if it was a good one, months later they would take credit for it. If it was a bad decision; of course, they could blame the others that made it. Well in this case, I imagine Secretary Cheny put the fear of God into the King's mind, because the next day, there were KC-10 USAF Tanker Refuelers sitting on the Royal Ramp of Riyadh airport. Within days there were Patriot missile batteries guarding that airport also.

Well, within weeks the leaders of organizations returned from their vacations, and reviewed the plans made by the #2 leaders in their absence. I must say, my feelings toward these leaders fell to a low point, as they criticized my plans for communications and other plans in response to possible Scud attacks on Riyadh. They felt I overreacted to this threat, since the Scud did not have a range to reach Riyadh that we knew of. I believed my military and engineering background was such that their belittling of my efforts was a low blow. Greg then asked me to extend my assignment with EDC till December. With his lack of support for my plans, and my past extension of a year already, and with Nedra sent home overnight after the invasion, I told Greg that an extension was out of the question. Besides, President Bush by then set Jan 15th of

1991 as the target date to invade Kuwait and push Saddam out, which made my decision more firm.

There are many stories of the invasion period that I recall. Many were heartwarming, and courageous. One such story involved the AT&T people stuck in their Holiday Inn Hotel in Kuwait after the Iraq invasion. There was a worker in Bill Postma's team at WESA (Western Electric of Saudi Arabia) that was a retired Army Msgt. He was asked by the Chief of AT&T if there was any way he could get our people out of Kuwait with the Iraqi Army all over the place. He took the mission on and was given a roll of money to do it. He drove to Dhahran and recruited a Saudi friend that knew the terrain and towns around Kuwait City. They hired a school bus and drove to the Kuwaiti/Saudi border. There, the AT & T retired Army NCO stopped a Kuwaiti that just drove out of the border via a desert route if the cell phone in his Mercedes worked? He said "yes" and further said "the phone system in Kuwait City was still working too." He bought the cell phone for $300 and pulled it out of the car and put it into the bus he had. His friend drove into Kuwait in a pick-up truck, as he talked to the AT&T workers in their hotel. He convinced some of them to follow his plan, which was to get out of the hotel, go to car rental places, or their own cars, and follow his friend across the desert to the border. There he would take them by bus back to Riyadh. If any cars got stuck enroute, they were to keep getting into other cars still running as needed to get across the border.

About half the people made it, and he got them to Riyadh safely. He was told to go back to try to get the rest of the crew. He did so, and after days of talking on the cell phone, convinced the rest to follow the same plan, and get across the border to safety. He succeeded again. I asked my friend Bob Postma, if the retired Sgt. got a fair reward for his heroism and plan. The man was a temporary employee of AT & T and I think he wanted permanent status with AT & T if possible. I don't know for sure, but I think the Dutch Leader of the AT & T group did not give the rescuer a fair reward. Sad but true.

Another small factor of the war time period involved a MASH type hospital just down the road from our office on the Riyadh airbase. I wanted to see if it matched the MASH field hospitals depicted on the MASH TV series. One day I drove to the hospital area, and showed the guard my retired Military ID. He allowed me in, and YES, it was a perfect replica of the MASH unit hospitals we saw on TV.

CHAPTER FIFTEEN: BACK HOME AGAIN—AND AGAIN

After a period of respite, Frank reported for duty at S & P. His services weren't needed in the final phases of the Peace Shield project, and the reception around the job was cool. At his annual review, Frank received a zero percent raise. His VP, Mr. Biel said this was based largely upon the fact that he had received greater than average raises while in Saudi. Nevertheless, it became apparent that his services as an engineer were no longer needed, and he sought out a position in another portion of the company, marketing the company's services to government contractors, and other hi-tech businesses that might need high-level engineering projects. Soon, he was dealt another blow.

I looked into the chances of going back to the Industrial Division that allowed me to move to the Saudi Project over three years ago. I found that, like my situation across the street with the Architectural Division, the work level in Industrial was light, and my chances of being offered a position there were nil. I was told that a newer Division called Advanced Technology was a spin-off of the Special Structures Section that did the Space Shuttle Project at Vandenburg AFB was growing, and that there may be an opportunity for me there. I interviewed with Larry Leonard, the new VP of Advanced Technologies shortly. He was a former Mechanical Engineer with the Industrial Division, and I recall knowing him slightly. We met soon, and he told me that he could use a new assistant in marketing the projects for the Division. Although I never worked in marketing, I felt sure that I could do the work, so I volunteered to go to work for him. I started in early 1991 and got busy trying to establish contacts with the agencies and companies that could use the services of the Advanced Technology Div. I soon found out that we were competing head-to-head with our own Advanced Technology Group located at Tullahoma, TN. I started writing letters of introduction and scheduling trips to meet engineers at Lockheed for the F-22 project, Cape Kennedy for vehicle launch projects, Martin-Marietta for Missile Launch projects, and many such firms and projects. Since I was the new kid-on-the-block, my receptions were usually lukewarm, and meetings with contacts were cool and short. What I didn't know, was that Larry Leonard was in hot water with the big officers in our own Corporation since these type projects were on the back burner in most companies, and that a replacement for Larry, from

Government Offices in Washington was about to be hired.

On the home front, I was still busy with some volunteer work I was doing before our Saudi assignment. One such effort involved my blood platelet donation for the Red Cross at Barnes Hospital on Kings Highway near downtown St. Louis. My platelet count was always high, at over 500,000/platelet per donation. In blood donation terms, I was a double-digiter, which meant I filled two bags each visit. They loved donors like me, since it was like two persons giving at once. I had been donating these components of my blood for over 10 years, by this time.

In addition to donating platelets, I noted that a doctor at Barnes was heading a study in men, seeking an easy way to diagnose prostate cancer in its early stages. I had a benign prostate growth in the mid-80's that was operated on by a young doctor at Christian Hospital NE. Since the PSA Study tests were being done free at Barnes hospital, I decided to do the tests while I was there for my platelet donations. The first test, which was comprised of a rectal finger exam and a four-sector needle biopsy, was done in the fall of 1991. The test was negative, and I was elated, except for the fact that one of the four quadrant biopsies was *lost*. I called the hospital and asked what we should do next. Their suggestion was to wait three months for the needle contamination to clear the area, and redo the tests again in December. I agreed to do that.

A redo of the PSA test series was done, and in days a Doctor of the screening group called to inform me that the test was POSITIVE. What a Shocker. Nedra didn't believe it, and went into denial. Being a fatalist, like many pilots, I thought the results were correct and started to make plans for the next course of action. I had switched to another doctor named Fathman in the St. Louis Urological Group earlier, when my younger doctor left our company's

Insurance group. Dr. Fathman had a super bedside manner, and I was real happy with the switch I had made. I consulted with him about my PSA results, and he quickly recommended prostate removal by surgery. The only problem was that he no longer worked out of Christian Hospital Northeast, but only out of their St. Lukes Hospital in West County. He did agree that if I took all my office visits out West, he would come back east to our closer hosp. for the surgery. This was not a major problem for us, and we set a surgery date for January of 1991.

With my prostate surgery pending, and our new VP on station, it became readily apparent to me that I should consider early retirement soon. I discussed this option with an old friend, now a VP named Ron Williams. He advised me, that if we could afford it, this was a great option to consider. He said that projects were slow all over the Corporation and that a smooth departure on our own terms was a highly recommended thing to do. Nedra and I talked it over, and decided that after the operation we would retire early in late February. We told the new Division VP and he was happy with our decision. I am sure it saved him the problem of letting me go, sooner or later, and likely sooner.

As a former attorney specializing in employment discrimination, especially age-related discrimination, it's obvious to me that Frank was a victim. Nevertheless, it's also obvious to me that Frank was ripe for retirement—a real retirement, this time.

The biggest blessing of the surgery was that with

timely healing, and the rapid diagnosis of early-on cancer of the prostate led to a rapid recovery, with a zero PSA, and a healthy outlook, that has held up very, very well. I passed my annual flight physicals ever since, although the first one after Surgery required a nice letter from my surgeon, before the FAA would pass me in 1992. Of course I did experience some post-surgery side effects, but with Dr. Fathmans consultations, an understanding and helpful Nedra all the way, and lots of humor, our life after cancer has turned out just super.

One side effect of early retirement was a lot of new planning for vacations and relaxation trips. After Saudi, we decided that our vacations would involve domestic trips and places, so we could understand the conversations and recognize the food when it was served. We heard from ladies at morning mass that the Lone Oak Resort in the western Lake-of-theOzarks was a nice place to fish (Nedra's favorite sport), swim, and relax. We tried it one summer, and ended up going there about four times, and loving it more each time. We enjoyed a SAC Air Force bomber crew reunion twice, and plan more of those vacations.

Our retirement to Florida started slowly, as our Hospice volunteer friends Pat & Fred Dick told us of this super friendly mobile home park in Southwestern FL just east of Bradenton, FL, in a small town called Ellenton. They suggested we look it over, and we checked on condos and apartments in the area. They had been going there since Pat was a little girl, in her parents travel trailer. We couldn't find a reasonable place to rent in the high season of December of '93, so Pat & Fred offered us a week in their nice mobile home at 196 Denmark Drive. This was a first for them, since they customarily only let family stay in their winter home.

The Dick's tale of really friendly neighbors was surely true, and I stopped near all the "For Sale" homes I listed to try and find out what the home sale deals were all about. As luck would have it, we stopped near the home for sale at 187 Denmark and chatted with the neighbors Dot and Ed Smith who live next door. We told Dot & Ed that we really preferred a rental, since we were not sure how this commuting and snow bird lifestyle would agree with us. They told us that their neighbors Peg and Steve O'Sullivan of Connecticut who live winters at 185 Denmark lost their winter renter due to illness, and that we should meet them in 2 hours as they return from the Friendship Hall swimming pool. As it turns out further chats with the Smiths revealed that Ed worked at the Sverdrup & Parcel Boston office in the past, while I worked at S & P's Head Office Location in St. Louis, MO. A really small world, isn't it?

The home next door at 187 Denmark Dr. had been rented for the winter for $1200 plus utilities to a Michigan couple. Since it was for sale, they had to let us view it, and we asked the Colony Cove realty agency if we could look it over? They agreed and we looked at it about Jan 15th or so. The home was a bit darker inside than our rental but the porch view of the riverside was great. The only problem was that the porch was only 12 feet across, but Nedra saw the potential of extending it across the full width of the double wide unit. Within a few minutes of seeing it, Nedra said "I want this home." Decisive me, said "you have it" within seconds of her request. We told the renters of our plans, and they reminded us that they had it rented till March 30th. We understood, and started plans to make an offer to buy it. A nice feature is that this home is moved forward on a small peninsula at the juncture of the marina channel and the river. That means that from the porch side, you don't see any other mobile units, which yields a privacy that few others in the park enjoy.

One funny story came out of when I ran for Colony Cove HOA President. I felt as if not enough Snowbirds were being represented on the Board, so I ran. Well, on the day of the election, as the election results were announced, the Secretary had a hard time pronouncing a winner's name as "Fran ???, and I thought that had to be me. Since I couldn't hear very well without my hearing aids, and the Secretary's difficulty with the name, I was sure it was me. After the announcements were done, the President asked for comments from the audience, and I stood up and announced my "Thanks for my election" and was surprised when the current Board got up, almost en mass, to say, "It wasn't you that got elected, but Fran Abbey." I was embarrassed to say the least, and then told the crowd "thanks all for not electing me."

Later that year, the President of CCMHOA invited me to a Board meeting of CCMHOA. After announcing that the elected Vice-President submitted his resignation for personal reasons, Herb Ferrand asked me if I was still interested in serving. I said yes, and the Board accepted my offer. The President asked me to leave for a few minutes, and they then proceeded to make me their Vice-President, if I would accept, which I did. I went from an unelected Board Officer to Vice-President of CCMHOA in one easy lesson.

Retirement did little to staunch Frank's pace. He eagerly became affiliated with the Experimental Aircraft Association (EAA) chapter 180, based in Sarasota, Florida at the Sarasota-Bradenton International Airport (SRQ, in aviation speak). Among many other duties, the EAA chapter is responsible for managing a program known as the Young Eagles, with members providing free introductory flights to children. Frank had bought a private airplane known as a Mooney, a single-engine, low-wing high-performance aircraft, and he utilized this airplane to give 653 youngsters their first airplane flight.

Frank loves the Mooney, but had some initial questions about one particular part and procedure:

I scheduled a dual flight at Cirrus Aviation School at the Dolphin FBO Building. I checked out in their C-172 last year, and the Chief Pilot remembered me and told me that a flight to learn the "Johnson Bar" would be easy, since all his pilots fly their Mooney, which has the bar. He said it's all in the wrist motion, and then we set up a flight for 2 PM on a Wednesday in November. Nedra was to work as a consultant at Kelly Sew/Vacuum Shop that day. I dropped Nedra off at 1100 hrs, and proceeded to SRQ and the Jones FBO ramp where my Mooney N7106U is tied down. I read in an old MAPA magazine of a certain spar corrosion location to check for. I polished another 1/8th of the plane, and checked in particular for the spar corrosion area. The plane looked good, and I completed a good preflight inspection and taxied from the Jones ramp the Dolphin ramp, Cirrus Aviation and my instructor. I was early, and I asked the Cirrus dispatcher if my instructor was available for an early departure? She said he was in the lobby for lunch, and I went there to chat with him. He is a Frenchman from the Lesser Antilles islands, and we chatted for a few minutes. He was done with a light lunch, and he explained the Johnson Bar wrist motion techniques, and we proceeded to the aircraft for flight. The engine start went smoothly, and we taxied to runway 14 for take-off. The wind was from 220 degrees so we had a right cross-wind for take-off. My first lift of the "Johnson Bar" went so smoothly, that I couldn't believe it. We departed to the south for some slow flight, and more Johnson Bar practice. All in all, I started to have some trouble locking the gear in the "up" position. We returned to Sarasota/Bradenton airport (SRQ) for some touch-and-go landing practice. We did three landings, and I squeaked them all in. After the flight my instructor, Ulysses, noted that my Johnson Bar worked much harder than the unit in their (Cirrus) Mooney. He looked around the floor of the aircraft and showed me where the rug in the base area of the Johnson Bar could be causing some interference in the locking of the bar in the Gear Up position. I had Nedra help me clear that rug problem, and my fears of "the Bar" and the aircraft disappeared.

Additionally, Frank participated in the Civil Air Patrol (CAP), which is a civilian auxiliary of the USAF. The CAP is much like ROTC, where young people interested in the Air Force are provided the opportunity to become acquainted with military life and the duties of the USAF. Primarily, CAP assists civilian authorities in searching for downed civil aircraft. This fine organization is always in need of experienced leadership, which Frank obviously provided. However, in Florida, the CAP "High Bird" Missions involve something else.

In Florida, our Squadron, FL044, has a C-172 and our support of the C/N missions largely involves surveillance of the coastal waters for immigration violations and possible large boat to smaller boat drug deal handoffs. We recently (1999) started to get involved with a high bird mission in support of the DOD. We would pick up a "Mission Impossible" type of young Air Force Special Forces man with a full load of heavy radio gear. He would fill up the back seat with his gear, and install special antennae on the plane side windows, for contact with the DOD Controllers at MacDill and Tyndall Air Force bases. Another CAP plane (a Cessna 310 Twin engine bird) would go West on a special flight plan and descend below the radar screen of the Air Defense Identification Zone (ADIZ).

The C-310 would then fly Eastbound, as an unidentified "intruder" into the US ADIZ area. There are high flying tethered balloons at 15,000 ft. near Key West and Cross City on the Florida West coast. These balloons contain radar gear to detect such intruding planes and extend the radar horizon for such needs. These radar contacts would alert USAF controllers and set up an airborne interception mission. Our back seat passenger would talk with local and distant USAF controllers to stay abreast of the impending intercept mission.

Our job as High Bird is to establish contact with the low flying CAP C-310 and provide a safety net for guarding his location in the event of a ditching in the Gulf of Mexico. At 10,000 ft loiter altitude, we can easily stay in contact with the crew at all times. The back seat operator keeps us aware of all USAF Controller actions such as an F-16 formation (usually 2 planes) for the intercept mission. We then keep the C-310 aware of the proximity of the intercept fighters, and them aware of the appearance of the C-310 they are intercepting. Thus the safety of the mission is enhanced.

For the High Bird crew it is mostly a boring "holding pattern" type mission, but the chatter as the fighters launch and start the intercept mission, it is an adrenalin charged time. Of course we are on our toes all the time since we all realize what a vital safety net we provide the low flying CAP plane and crew during these missions. After a short break for refueling and a sandwich, we do it all over again. Recently we started using a nearby units C-182, since their long range fuel tanks make for a longer "on station" time so necessary for better mission support. We are really "charged up" when the Air Force members and our intruder plane crews pass on their "thanks" for a job well done. For many of us former military flight crews, this is a double adrenalin charge, since this closely replicates many of our active duty mission profiles.

Meanwhile, Nedra was becoming frustrated; her children were grown and gone, and she had spent so much of her life supporting her husband, tending to the children, and keeping the home. Another thing that brought her great pleasure, however, was sewing. Therefore, when they retired and Frank kept up his variety-of-projects lifestyle, Nedra acquired a number of sewing and embroidery machines and spent hours each day making dynamic clothing, crafts, and anything else that could be made with fabric and thread. Her benevolent soul found ways to meet clothing needs, even when not asked to do so. As mentioned earlier, Nedra made countless "wheelchair" blankets for veterans at the VA hospital in Bay Pines, Florida.

Oddly enough, after having spent great portions of time separated for so many years, once Frank and Nedra had the opportunity to spend time together, they did so, but also continued the pattern that had been established, respecting one another as individuals and giving one another space.

In the spring of 2013, however, Nedra proposed an idea that was somewhat out of character.

CHAPTER SIXTEEN:
ENGINEERING AN EXIT

Everyone with whom I spoke—those who knew Nedra anyway—said virtually the same thing: Nedra knew her time was running out. Afflicted with COPD for some time, Nedra—not surprisingly—downplayed the disease and responded by continuing her cigarette habit. After all, her mother, Wannie, "had a six pack of 905 and two packs of cigarettes a day and lived to be almost 80." Mary Kimberlin, Nedra's sister-in-law, remembers speaking with Nedra not long before her death. "She said the doctor had diagnosed her with COPD and Heart Disease and she told me, 'It doesn't bother me,' but I knew that it did. I could hear it in her voice.

People recall Nedra having a "sixth sense," or at the very least, a deep intuition about things, and all are convinced that Nedra knew. Moreover, she even planned the whole thing.

First of all, she insisted that they go on an open-ended vacation to St. Louis of "three weeks or so," without any return plans or tickets purchased. This was late spring of 2013, and many opine that this was Nedra's way of being closer to her children when she passed away. Steven said, "The only reason they ever came to St. Louis was for marriages, births and deaths. Why they came this time, out of season, none of us had any earthly idea. Obviously, looking back, she had her reason."

Frank recalls that she was further pleased to note that Jeanne was "ok that Ross had moved out and that Claire would be coming home. Jeanne was Nedra's utmost concern, because of a number of issues, but mostly because of her ongoing health issues. Nedra and Jeanne spoke frequently. Believing Jeanne to be doing well would be a great comfort to Nedra.

Additionally, Nedra suggested she and Frank stay at a hotel, rather than one of the children's homes. Each of those I interviewed insisted this out-of-character move was evidence that Nedra knew she was going to die, and that she did not wish to do so at the home of one of her children. They checked into the Hollywood Hotel and Casino and, on the night of June 21st—the summer solstice and longest day of the year—Nedra scored big at the casino, netting about $1,500! In the wee hours of the following morning, Frank went to check on her and found her at eternal peace.

This "sudden exit" also seemed contrived, as many of those who knew Nedra admit that, had she endured a lengthy, lingering death, Nedra would have taken it upon herself to console her visitors!

After a lifetime of management, organization, support,

253 | DANCING IN THE STRATOSPHERE

----

encouragement, and doing for others, Nedra, who once confessed to Steven that her greatest fear was that Frank would pass on before her, embraced her destiny and made her own passing as easy on her loved ones as humanly possible.

Afterword

Frank Szachta is a remarkable man, who overcame obstacles and enjoyed fortune along his journey to somehow meet the only woman on the planet who was up for the challenge of being Mrs. Frank Szachta; who had the good fortune of being introduced to aviation at an early age, to be thrust into joining the Air Force and encouraged by Nedra to seek a commission and, ultimately, pilot training.

Born without an "Off" switch, Frank has moved through his life with velocity and road map. When Nedra passed on, he was suddenly without "my engine and my rudder." Understandably, Frank was concerned that losing the hub of his family would send the children in all directions of the compass. Truth is, they had already gone their separate ways, although most held a firm grasp on the tether that lead to their mother.

Frank and Nedra walked the journey in the same fashion; often separated by distance, they held fast to the invisible chain that drew them together on the YWCA dance floor that St. Louis summer of '51. They blossomed in a time in American history when so much about life was simple, and when anything seemed possible.

Today, as Frank moves on without Nedra, there are times when he sees something that reminds him of her, and his mind will travel the distance to a memory. When it returns to the present, Frank feels the emptiness, the void, and he doesn't try to hide his sadness.

Only a few weeks ago, however, Frank awakened around 4:30 in the morning, opened his eyes, and there she was! A vision of his angel, Nedra. The moment came and went, but it provided Frank with a sense of peace, and a knowledge that they will one day be reunited.

As for the children, each is forging onward, each has his or her own set of challenges, of successes, of dreams. And each will always be proud of their father, and thankful for the mother who propelled them on their own individual journeys.

And for the Air Force, I'm sure it's faring fine without the likes of Major Frank Szachta; but I'll bet the farm those YWCA dances aren't the same.

ABOUT THE AUTHORS

Major Frank D. Szachta, USAF (Ret.), makes his home in Ellenton, Florida, overlooking the Manatee River. He spends his time involved in his church, his community and his friends, and still loves flying every chance he gets.

Wendell W. Thorne is a freelance writer who lives in Ellenton, Florida.

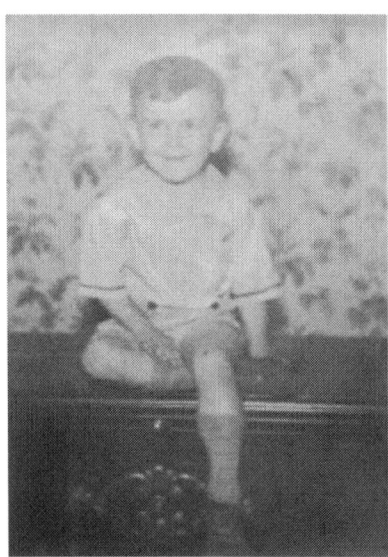

Nedra and Frank, all smiles

Nedra and her siblings

School Days

Burgard Vocational High School, Buffalo

Steen Aero Built by students of Buffalo's Burgard Vocational High School under supervision of Greg Ductor and Stan Fliss.

"Tent City" barracks at San Antonio's Lackland AFB, circa 1950

Early Pilot Training

Nedra the New Mom

The Green Hornet

AT-6 Texan Trainer at Bartow AFB

Frank and Nedra on their wedding day

*Above: T-33 Training Aircraft over Greeneville, MS;
Below: B-25 Mitchell Bomber*

B-47 Bomber at maximum takeoff power. Note the JATO collar on the aft underside of the fuselage.

C-47 "Goonie Bird" on the tarmac at Pease AFB, New Hampshire

McClellan AFB, Sacramento 1

Nedra and the kids, Washington

Frank, the Center of attention in Saudi

Frank on the wing of the Mooney

The Ever-buoyant Nedra

The Szachta Family. Back row, l-r, Bob, Evelyn, Frankie,
Steve; Front row, l-r, Carol, Nedra, Frank and Jeanne

Made in the USA
Charleston, SC
06 November 2015